My USA Adventures

Book Details

Epicentre Equilibrium Publishing

Copyright © 2012 by Leigh-Chantelle
Cover and Design by Adele Walker (www.adelewalker.blogspot.com)
Author Portrait by Carol Slater Photography (www.c-s-p.com.au)
Lettering: Leigh-Chantelle

Thanks to various friends for taking the photos on the cover

ISBN 978-0-9808484-2-7
www.epicentreequilibrium.com

About the Book

This is a collection of the blogs I wrote when travelling to the United States of America for the first time (as an adult) in 2010 and the second time in 2011. I worked for a couple of years organising and promoting my all-vegan, environmental-awareness *Green Earth Festival* that took place for the first time in Brisbane, Australia in March 2010. After this, my plan was either to travel around Australia or to go to South East Asia for a few months. I had never really thought about going to America. We'd been before as a family when I was younger, though I didn't remember much of it. But after deciding to speak at an Animal Rights conference in Washington, DC, I embarked on my mission to make some new friends and network around the US. I left for my first adventures in June 2010, had an amazing time, met a lot of like-minded people and made some life-long friends. I hadn't really planned on returning in 2011, but ended up doing just that in July and August.

After my second festival, *Green Earth Day* in March 2011, I decided not to continue to organise the event as it took over ever aspect of my life, completely. I now have my life back and am not willing to give it up anytime soon. With having a Sagittarian Sun (Star) sign I have travel in my bones and in my blood. For the first ten years of my life I lived on a tropical island: Bougainville Island in Papua New Guinea with my family, and we travelled overseas somewhere new each year when my Dad had time off from work. It was great, though I don't remember a lot of the places we travelled to. Fortunately, I work with Social Media and run my own company, therefore I can travel anywhere I want to now as long as I have WIFI connection and my laptop. I do love this and am very grateful to be working in an area I love. Actually, anything to do with communication in all its forms I enjoy.

This book is a text version of the blogs on the Updates section of my vivalavegan.net website that you can find here: vivalavegan.net/community/updates.html In the future, I will be releasing photo books of the photo from my blogs of my animal friends and my food photographs, as I have a lot of people who loved seeing these. I had a wonderful time on my US adventures in 2010 and 2011. I hope you enjoy hearing about the people and animals I met, the vegan restaurants I visited and the food I ate, the events I spoke at and all the places that I travelled to. I have now been to 14 out of 50 of the states in America. I will be working on adding more states to the list when I head back in 2013.

Thank you to all of the amazing people who are fans of mine, *Viva la Vegan!* and/or *Green Earth Group*. Thank you to those who follow my blogs, videos, interviews, articles, Social Media sites and the people whom I've been conversing with online or via email for years. It was great to meet a lot of these people in person. It's especially great when the people who inspire you are actually genuinely decent people, and humbling when they are inspired by you just as much.

Thank you to Adele Walker who is my go-to gal for anything design-related. Adele sprinkles her fairy dust of digital artistry over so many of my projects to make my work truly shine.

I am fortunate to know a lot of people in this wonderful world and I am grateful that I call a lot of them friends. Thank you to my life-long US friends who I miss incredibly when I am not in your presence – you know who you are.

Leigh-Chantelle

2010
june & july

US adventures part 1: Los Angeles, California

MONDAY 21 June: Beverly Hills, Santa Monica, 30 Days and Real Food Daily

To begin my US adventures, Adele and I had a sleep over the night before and she took me to the airport the next day. Cam met us there to say goodbye. My flight left at 11:00 on Monday June 21. The 13 hour flight wasn't that bad. The plane was completely full. I will be sending a feedback email to the airline I flew with, as they don't seem to know the difference between a vegan and a vegetarian. Why is this so hard? I had a pasta meal, bread roll and cooked vegetables - right next to scrambled *eggs*! - as one of my three meals on the way to Los Angeles. Not as good as Qantas vegan meals.

I arrived at LAX airport at 7:00 Monday 21 June so I had another Monday to live through, but I will lose two days when I return to Brisbane. The airport wasn't as big or as busy as I had heard it would be, customs etc wasn't a problem either. There was just a lot of waiting around. I was pretty exhausted as I'd slept a bit on the flight but not too much. Plus Adele and I had stayed up very late the night before I left. I had watched the movie, *A Single Man* with Colin Firth and Julianne Moore, actors I love and had flicked through a few programmes on the flight as well as listening to my own tunes on shuffle - love the shuffle button - is there anything better? The weather in LA was not as summery as I had hoped, it was overcast, windy and I was still wearing my scarf and jumper, my Brisbane Winter weather attire.

At the LAX airport I was told to look for a blue *Super Shuttle* bus that would take me to my hotel in Beverly Hills, these buses came past quite regularly but not to where I was heading. It seemed to take forever to get a bus and then to finally arrive at my hotel, as there were other people on the bus getting dropped off at their hotels before me. I arrived at the *Cresent Hotel*, a lovely little place, and checked in a lot earlier than the 15:00 regular check in time. Because I was checking in early the only room ready was the one closest to the entry/exit but I wasn't too concerned. I put all my belongings in my tiny room and headed out to wander around Beverly Hills for a bit.

I had to get a SIM card for my mobile phone when I was here so I headed to *T-Mobile* where I got a US$50 card which gives me unlimited text and calls within the US, plus US$25 for international texts. I contacted my *FaceBook* friend, Holly Brown who would be my LA tour guide and let my family and friends know that I'd arrived safely. There was a salad place next door to *T-Mobile*, so I got a takeaway meal there and wandered around a bit more. I found a great place to get a vegetable juice: *M cafe de Chaya,* that I found out later from Holly is a mostly vegan place with amazingly presented scarlet quinoa (!) salad, other salads and great cakes. I planned to return here for breakfast one morning but this never happened. I headed back to my hotel, had a rest for a few hours and then Holly picked me up and we headed off to Santa Monica.

We went to a great place for dinner, *Real Food Daily,* they also have a restaurant in West Hollywood. Holly and I ordered Not-chos to share: tortilla chips, melted cashew cheese, black beans, pico de gallo (uncooked tomato, onions etc), guacamole, tofu sour cream US$11.75. This was a great dish and really enough for us, but of course Holly had also ordered a salad for her and I had ordered nori maki for myself which was US$6.95 for 5 pieces and consisted of sweet brown rice, shiso, tempeh, avocado, carrot, collard greens, umeboshi (Japanese fruit), tamari dipping sauce, wasabi and pickled ginger.

We were very full after this so we didn't have room for any dessert, which is breaking the first rule of being a vegan. *Real Food Daily* is a great place to go if you are trying to make an impression, so take someone here on a first date or for something special. Our waiter was very courteous and friendly and though some may think the food is expensive it's worth the price you pay.

After dinner we headed to Holly's friend, Nik Tyler's place for a screening organised by another of their friends, Prabhat, who Holly said is like me in Brisbane because he is always organising vegan get togethers in LA. We were there to watch an episode from the series created by Morgan Spurlock, *30 Days*. The episode we watched was about the all-vegan Karpel family who welcomed a hunter into their house for a month. After the viewing, I ended up doing an interview with Melissa Karpel on the Santa Monica streets. Plus an interview with Nik who is one of the actors in the recently released animal rights movie, *Bold Native*.

TUESDAY 22 June: Animal Acres & Follow your heart

Much better weather today. The sun is out in LA so we will get on just fine! I wandered around Beverly Hills in the morning and headed to *Whole Foods* to get some muffins for my plane trip tomorrow. *Whole Foods* is similar to my home state, Queensland's *Mrs Flannery's* health food stores, but is obviously much larger with a huge amount of products. They still sell animals and animal products but there are a lot of healthier and ethical alternatives here. I also saw Kelly Rutherford who plays Lily (Serena's mum) on *Gossip Girl*, one of my favourite shows, so that was a bit exciting.

Holly had arranged for us to have a tour of the *Animal Acres* animal sanctuary, so we headed 45mins out of downtown LA around lunchtime to a place called Acton. We went through the San Fernando Valley and as Acton is in the desert, the weather was great. Mike was a wonderful tour guide and really amazing with the animals. He told us so many stories about the many animals at the sanctuary and I took some great photos.

I took some great video footage at *Animal Acres* and I had an interview with Mike as well as an interview with Erin and Cameron. It was a beautiful place to visit. I would recommend volunteering if you live in the area or having a guided tour one Sunday. There are also some great events that *Animal Acres* plan so check out their website. I'm also looking forward to meeting Lorri Houston, the founder of *Animal Acres*, and speaking with her and Alex Hershaft at the AR Conference in Washington, DC next month - we are speaking on Creating Effective Events.

We had worked up quite an appetite, so off Holly and I went to *Follow Your Heart* cafe in Canoga Park. *Follow Your Heart* are the creators of *Vegenaise* and they have a store attached to the cafe (or vice versa). The waiter was really friendly and came out with a sample of the dressings that *Follow Your Heart* create and sell in their store. Holly ordered a Club Sandwich, US$8.50. I had the Zorro Burrito: black beans, braised tofu, Jack and Cheddar cheese, Spanish rice and salsa wrapped in a tortilla and served with jicama Salad, guacamole and sour cream, US$10.50. My meal was great, but I had to take half with me to have later on for dinner.

We then went back to Holly's place for a few hours and watched *Behind the Mask,* a documentary Holly's friend, Shannon Keith released a few years ago that I hadn't seen before. This is about the *Animal Liberation Front* a group of people who rescue animals and never hurt other animals (including humans) in the process. There is an act in the USA called the *Animal Enterprise Terrorism Act* (AETA) that if you're not aware of, you should find out more about - it's pretty scary what the US government can do. Shannon has recently released a new movie on the fur industry, *Skin Trade*. I haven't watched this yet, but will let you know when I do. *Skin Trade* will be shown at the AR Conference in July.

I had a great time in LA with my friend Holly and was pleased to meet her other passionate vegan friends. Holly dropped me back at my hotel and I went to bed knowing I'd be in Portland, Oregon this time tomorrow!

US adventures part 2: Portland, Oregon & Let Live conference

WEDNESDAY 23 June: Portland, OR & Blossoming Lotus

I had organised the blue *Super Shuttle* to pick me up from my hotel in Beverly Hills and drive me to the airport for my flight at 13:25 to Portland, OR. I was picked up at 10:15 and we only had one couple to pick up en route to the airport. Waiting at the LAX airport is not fun at all.

There's no good food places, just the regular unhealthy, fat-laden rubbish that is everywhere nowadays. Why don't we have more choices than 4 similar "restaurants"? I thought I would wander around the airport for awhile as I like to do that at airports, but there wasn't much of an area to wander around in. So I ended up giving a few friends in the US a call, chatted to a lovely family from Eugene waiting at the airport and uploaded and edited my photos from LA.

My flight left at 13:25 and I arrived in Portland, Oregon at 15:40 and the weather was beautiful! My shuttle bus driver had said that it was raining in Portland on the trip to the airport and I was very impressed that the weather had cleared - especially for me. My good friend from Australia, Imber and her US husband Mark picked me up and we headed to *Blossoming Lotus* for a late lunch/early dinner.

We started off with Live Nachos US$9: spiced tomato & walnut chips, seasonal squash nacho cheese and taco crumbles topped with tomato, onion, cilantro (coriander), scallion (spring onion), cashew sour cream and avocado goddess sauce. This is a simply DIVINE dish! Mark and Imber shared the Oregon mushroom special. I had the Four Cheese Lasagna: layers of fresh seasonal vegetable marinara, semolina noodles, herbed tofu ricotta, roasted garlic & squash mozzarella, and sesame parmesan, served on a bed of steamed kale, topped with lemon-basil cashew cream US$14. Yum!

THURSDAY 24 June: Red & Black Cafe and Bold Native

We had a late lunch/early dinner at *The Red & Black Cafe* after Imber finished work. Imber & Mark both had the Black Dragon Noodles: wheat noodles, zesty peanut sauce, carrots, cilantro (coriander), sesame and lime US$5 and I had The Insurrectionist sandwich: house-made tempeh tuna salad, herbed veganaise, lettuce chiffonade (long thin strips) and shredded carrots US$6.25. Mark and I had a cupcake each as well US$2.50 each but I forgot to take a photo of them.

This place has a very grassroots, community, anti-establishment feel and the prices are great. They were out of a lot of additional items on the menu which wasn't good. Take someone here if you are on a budget, if you want to browse the great selection of books and if you or your meal date have eclectic taste.

After dinner Imber, Mark and I attended a viewing for *Bold Native* at the Portland University as part of the Let Live Conference. This movie was ten years in the making and the creators Denis Henry Hennelly & Casey Suchan answered questions afterwards along with a few cast members. This is a film that was created to inspire and create discussion, and is aimed mostly at an audience who already have some idea of animal rights and the *Animal Liberation Front*. Though it's in an easily-digestible format so that those who know not much about either can go along to see the film and hopefully find out more in the process. It's great to see some well-known vegan and animal rights people in the film and was great to see Nik Tyler & Erin in the film who I had interviewed a couple of days ago.

FRIDAY 25 June: Imber's birthday dinner at Portobello & Let Live launch

Imber, Mark and I headed to *Portobello* where my good friend from Brisbane, Jackson met us. Jackson's travelling around the West Coast of the USA on his motorbike at present so it was great to see him and spend some quality time together. *Portobello* is Imber's favourite restaurant thus a fitting place to take her on her birthday. Imber and Mark ordered chao cheese, apple, grapes and baguette as an entrée US$9.

I had the handmade linguine US$7 (half serve) which consisted of Red Pepper linguine, zucchini and corona beans. Jackson had Arraviata pizza that had vegan sausage on it. Mark and Imber ordered the ravioli. They also made me a great beet mocktail, very sweet but yum.

For dessert the birthday girl had a sundae: vanilla *Coconut Bliss* ice cream, chocolate sauce, hazelnuts and cherries US$6. Jackson had an Apple tart with Streusel topping (flour, sugar, cinnamon, salt & butter) and vanilla *Coconut Bliss* ice cream US$7 and I had an immensely divine Raw Chocolate Tart US$12.

There was a talk on by Andy Stepanian tonight as part of the pre-Let Live Conference that we had wanted to attend. We hadn't ordered our desserts until after Andy's talk was over, so we only caught a bit of the next event: the Spelling Bee when we arrived. Not my thing at all but there were a heap of people enjoying themselves.

SATURDAY 26 June: Let Live conference & Portobello

Today was the real start of the Portland Let Live conference at Portland University. There were around 30 tables from different Animal Rights groups. I made some great contacts, networked a lot and made some great new vegan friends. As I had a stall for *Viva la Vegan!* I didn't get to attend some of the great talks available throughout the day, but had a wander around the room and managed to check out the Farmers Markets downstairs for a bit when Jackson was looking after my stall. The Farmers Markets are great with quite a few vegan options. I had a dhal curry from one of the vendors. There were also bands and musicians playing and a lot of people gathering out in the sun!

Mark, Imber and I went to *Portobello* for dinner, in what most people thought was meant to be more of a standing, sociable occasion, but instead it was exactly the same as the night before, though a lot busier. At least there were some new options on the menu including Mark's pizza US$9 and my first taste of *Daiya* cheese. Imber and I both had the lasagne and I had Strawberry cheesecake for dessert US$6, though we were all disappointed when the raw chocolate tart I'd had the night before wasn't available.

Portobello is always busy with many people waiting for a table for hours. They've actually just moved into a bigger place as well. We didn't have to wait too long to get our table or meals, but it's been said that if you come after 7pm you will most likely have to wait for awhile. Some people have waited for 2 hours to get a table!

SUNDAY 27 June: Let Live conference & Bye and Bye Bar

Sunday was the last day of the Let Live conference, which was a great networking experience. The focus of the weekend was on creative activism and there seems to be a huge activism network in Portland. It's so great to meet people you've heard about or been friends with on FaceBook or MySpace for years. I did a few interviews with some of my new friends.

The wonderful Christopher Greenslate who with his partner released the book, *On a Dollar a Day*, about their experiences on living on US$1 a day. Christopher and his partner Kerri Leonard are both social justice teachers and Christopher has a lot to say about his book, veganism and other social justice issues such as the *Falling Whistles* campaign for peace.

Then I interviewed Rex Ray who runs *Vegan Threat* podcasts on veganism and how to get more active with promoting veganism. Rex also has a button making business and I look forward to seeing him and another new friend, Alex (who was tabling for Rex's button store) when I head to Seattle in a couple of weeks. Rex also interviewed me for his website.

Another great Seattle couple I met were Kirby Johnson and Anika Ledhe who run *Lions Share Industries*, a clothing company based in Seattle. Kirby and I had a great chat and interview. I ran out of time to interview Anika but hope to get the chance to when I see her and Kirby in Seattle. Anika runs a great Seattle blog: *Vegan Score.*

Last but not least, I also interviewed Daniel Tudor who is part of *Sparrow Media* a group consisting of Andy Stepanian (*SHAQ7*), Danielle Thompson (*Galapagus Preservation Society*) and Daniel. *Sparrow Media* are a promotion company focused on using creativity in its many forms to promote social, environmental, political and animal rights issues. You can find all these interviews on the *Viva la Vegan!* YouTube channel: youtube.com/vivalavegandotnet or on the Audio/Visual page on vivalavegan.net.

Mark, Imber and I then went to *Bye & Bye* vegan bar around 22:00 for dinner as the official closer to the Let Live conference. We all had these HUGE mocktails, served in a jar of all things. I ordered a simple brown rice, tofu and collared greens meal. Mark and Imber both had sandwiches. We were very tired when we went home for the night after our big weekend at the Let Live conference.

US adventures part 3: week 2 in Portland, Oregon

TUESDAY 29 June: Hungry Tiger Too

Tonight Imber, Mark and I went to dinner at *Hungry Tiger Too* for one of Imber's workmate's goodbye dinner. This isn't a vegan place but has a huge separate vegan menu and half of the space is a bar and the other is the restaurant.

Imber & Mark had Stuffed Wontons US$6 with roasted butternut squash and served with warm coconut milk and sweet chilli sauce. Mark had a Hawaii Five-O Burger US$9.75 that consisted of a *Boca* burger, grilled pineapple, soy mozzarella, lettuce, tomato, onion with teriyaki and garlic aioli and served with sweet potato fries. Imber had the Corn Dog Basket, which is two hot dogs dipped in batter and served with golden tots (potato gems) US$7.

I don't like deep fried food much at all, so I chose the healthiest item on the menu, the Tofu Skewers which I has assumed the tofu and the vegetables would be on skewers with each other, this however was served as a slab of tofu on one skewer and the vegetables on another, on a bed of savoury polenta US$6 (US$8 for two.)

Mark was deciding whether or not to have the cherry pie (US$4) that a couple of the other people at our table had ordered. It looked and tasted great, but Mark was too late as they had just served the last piece, so he missed out.

WEDNESDAY 30 June: Portland on foot & various food places

Today I decided to go into Portland city and wander around for the day. I was armed with instructions of what buses to catch and a map of the city. The buses from Lake Oswego where Imber and Mark live only go into the city between 06:12-09:02 & 15:43-17:57 and back from the city to Lake Oswego from 14:32 & 18:36. I caught the 9:02 bus, which got me into the city at about 09:30. I had a lovely bus companion: a lady studying Childhood Education as one of her boys has ADHD and the other is autistic. We had a great chat into the city.

I got off at SW Jefferson and 5th and walked up until the Oregon Historical Society and Portland Art Museum which I had thought I would check out, but both weren't open until 10:00 and I wasn't in the mood to wait around. So I headed up through the Farmers Markets until I got to SW Salmon Street, which I followed up West until I reached SW 18th Street. My main goals for the day were to get another phone card from *T-Mobile* for my international text messages and to go to *Powell's* bookstore, plus find some vegan places that Mark had suggested for me from the *Happy Cow* website.

So I walked North down SW 18th Street, past the Stadium where baseball and (US) football is played - the stadium is huge! Then I walked East down NW Glisan Street until I was around NW 3rd, 4th & 5th Streets where the vegan and vegetarian places are. Worked out that the closest one was going to be *Vegetarian House* so I walked South on NW 4th Street until I found the restaurant in China Town. This is a *Supreme Master Ching Hai Association* vegan restaurant, just like *Loving Hut* (my favourite) in Brisbane, so I was sure I would be fed well. There was an option to choose the buffet or order from the menu. I chose to have the buffet, which had fried rice, stir-fried vegetables, Textured Vegetable Protein (TVP), chilli and noodles, battered/deep friend sweet potato and broccoli. The meal was alright but not as good as Brisbane's *Loving Hut* but the buffet only cost US$7.

After lunch I walked along W Burnside Street until I found *Powell's* bookstore - WOW! *Powell's City of Books* is the largest used and new bookstore in the world, occupying an entire city block with more than a million new and used books in stock. The store has nine colour-coded rooms that house over 3,500 different sections. I looked in every section and this store is simply amazing. I spent a couple of hours wandering around, found a great Rhyming dictionary from 1960, hung out in the astrology section for an hour or so, bought a couple of astrology books - one from 1927! - and another study guide on *Wuthering Heights*, my favourite book. There is also a great record store, *Jackpot Records* on the same street that I checked out for a bit. I've worked in music stores most of my life, so it's always a good feeling to walk into one.

I started to walk back to where my bus stop was and met a great guy, Derek, who had lived in Portland most of his life but now lived overseas. He was here on holidays and as all his friends were at work, he was wandering around Portland taking photos. We wandered around for about an hour together, chatting like we were old friends. Derek gave me some tourist information and he left to eat his lunch at one of the parks. I had a bit of time until my bus arrived, so I decided I would go to another of the vegan places Mark had suggested and headed to *DC Vegetarian* on SW 3rd Avenue. *DC Vegetarian* is one of about 10 different street cart food vendors in this particular area. I bought a *Tofutti* mint chocolate ice cream sandwich for US$0.75 to eat now and a *Monkey Wrench* double chocolate cookie for later US$2. There is also a cart called *Sonny Bowl* that serve curries with quinoa and another cart for the *Portland Smoothie Company*, both of these are also vegan.

At the bus stop in the city to go back to Lake Oswego, I met a lovely 17-year old young lady who had just finished volunteering at one of the hospitals in the city. We had a great talk all the way home and I was excited to find out that her best friend is vegan, mostly raw and gluten free as well.

That night we went out for dinner with Mark's Animal Rights law lecturer, Steve Wise and some of Mark's classmates. Steve had decided we should go to *Vegetarian House* for dinner, so off I went again to China Town to eat. This time I ordered from the menu. Imber ordered spring rolls US$2.50 and Lemon Chicken US$12.95 which is similar to the one at *Pu Kwong* restaurant back in Brisbane. Mark ordered mixed tofu with vegetables US$8.95. I ordered the mixed vegetable chow mein with tofu US$7.50. My meal had way too many noodles, I pretty much picked out all the vegetables and left the noodles for Mark to finish. We weren't really impressed with the meals, but I don't think you can do better than their lunch buffet for US$7!

THURSDAY 1 July: Blossoming Lotus & Skin Trade

The lovely Jackson came to visit Lake Oswego from Eugene where he's been staying. We were meant to go for a ride on his motorbike but as it had been overcast, cold and raining most of the afternoon, we decided to wait to see if the weather would be better tomorrow. Imber, Mark, Jackson and I went to *Blossoming Lotus* for dinner. We didn't get to the restaurant until about 8pm and the place was full, plus there were people waiting to be seated, about 4 couples or groups in front of us. So we ordered some drinks and waited patiently for about 30 mins, though it seemed longer to me. I ordered the Lavender Lemondade US$3, Jackson had the Berry Fusion US$7, Mark had the Coconut Kauai Chai US$4 and Imber had the Thai Greens US$8.

I have decided that *Blossoming Lotus* is my favourite vegan place in Portland to eat. The staff are very friendly and helpful, the meals are delicious and the place has a great atmosphere. Jackson and I shared the Live Nachos as did Mark and Imber - these are amazing! - US$9 each.

By the time we got our main meals it was about 10pm and we weren't as hungry as we were in the beginning. I ordered the Live Wrap US$10, ate half and took the other two wraps home for lunch tomorrow. Jackson ordered the BBQ Tempeh platter US$12 that came with a side salad. Mark had the Seasonal Stir-fry US$12. Imber had the White Lotus soup US$6 and the Crispy Thai BBQ salad US$13.

When we got back to Imber and Mark's, Jackson and I watched *Skin Trade* the latest documentary from Shannon Keith who runs *Uncaged Films* and *ARME*. *Skin Trade* is about the Fur trade and how the fur industry is trying to promote their "products" as ethical and environmentally friendly. Shannon has done a great job with the documentary. There are interviews with celebrities, undercover footage as well as some cute animation. This is a really great documentary, and though there are obviously some graphic scenes, it's not too graphic of a documentary and one that everyone should watch. The upcoming AR Conference in Washington, DC will also be showing *Skin Trade* on the Saturday night.

FRIDAY 2 July: Motorbike adventures & Mt Hood National Park

Most mornings in Lake Oswego start with a green smoothie made in Mark & Imber's *Blendtec* blender, that until I used it I did not believe that it would actually blend to a smooth consistency. This morning I made Mark, Jackson and I a green smoothie with various green leaves in the fridge, carrots, and walnuts. Jackson and I also had one each of my left over Live Wrap meal from last night at *Blossoming Lotus.*

Mark then took Jackson and I on a tour of the *Lewis & Clark* law school where Mark is studying Animal Law and where Jackson is planning on sitting in on a course or giving a guest lecturer next year. Jackson lectures on Animal Law at Bond University at the Gold Coast, back home. Jackson also practices Entertainment Law and was one of my star volunteers at the *Green Earth Festival* I organised in March in Brisbane. The *Lewis & Clark* law school is very tranquil and lush. We also visited the Manor House, which was gorgeous. Mark is a great tour guide!

It was a bit wet in the morning but after our tour of the law school campus the sun came out, so Jackson and I decided we would go on a motor bike ride. Before we left, I made a simple sandwich for Mark, Jackson and I that consisted of *Alvarado Street Bakery* Sprouted Rye bread, *Wild Wood Organics* Sproutofu veggie burgers and *Galaxy Nutritional Foods* vegan mozzerella cheese slices. Then Jackson and I were on our way.

We went through quite a few places including Damascus, Estacada and Mt Hood National Forest. We stopped along the way in a few areas to stretch our legs and eat *Larabars* which are delicious, raw, gluten free, vegan bars mostly made up of 4 ingredients. We had the Lemon bar that consists of dates, cashews, almonds and lemon as well as the Chocolate Cherry made up of organic dates, organic almonds, organic walnuts, organic unsweetened cherries, Fair Trade-certified organic cocoa powder and cocoa mass. These bars are divine!

We stopped at a lil' town (I think it was Estacada) to get some snacks for our trip: some more bars, fruit, juices and chips. Jackson and I stopped at a lovely place, Timothy Lake to eat at around 8pm and it was absolutely FREEZING! I had so many layers on and Jackson's jacket, he didn't have much to keep him warm at all. We couldn't have been any colder and our fingers were like ice.

On the drive back to Lake Oswego it started to rain. It wasn't that bad in the beginning, but then it started to pour and it was truly scary when going down the mountain slopes on the bike. We pulled over a couple of times but then when the fog appeared and Jackson couldn't see in front of him, we turned around to a place we'd just passed and decided to stay at a lovely place called *Mt Hood Inn*, right at the bottom of Mt Hood.

Dinner that night was from *Ice Axe Grill*, the place next door to where we were staying. I wasn't venturing out in the cold anymore, so Jackson went next door to see what vegan fare they had. We shared The Buehler Burger US$10.75 a house made lentil burger with cucumber, arugula (rocket), tomatoes, stone ground mustard sauce on a 9 grain bun, with chips and a side salad - it was actually quite good. Then we thawed out.

SATURDAY 3 July: Motorbike adventures & Mt Hood

Jackson and I started the morning with breakfast of one banana each and half a Chocolate Mint *Larabar.* Since we were right at the foot of Mt Hood, Jackson and I headed to the tip. With an altitude of 11,249 feet (3,429 m) we were right at the top of Oregon's highest mountain and it was truly beautiful. We stopped at *Timberline Lodge* where we wandered around the lodge, played badminton, and Jackson played the piano while I played Shuffleboard with some of the kids.

Then we headed back to Lake Oswego. It was a beautiful experience to be amongst nature and on my first 2-day motorbike adventure with the lovely Jackson. There are so many beautiful spots throughout Mt Hood National Park, to drive, cycle, walk or camp, so make sure you check it out next time you're in the area.

Before Jackson left to head back to Eugene, I made us both a double-decker sandwich on *Alvarado Street Bakery* Sprouted Rye bread that consisted of Greek Olive & Roasted garlic Hummus, avocado and *Wild Food organics* Royal Thai Baked Sproutofu for the bottom layer; and *Galaxy Nutritional Foods* vegan mozzerella cheese slices, strawberries and baby spinach leaves for the top layer – yum.

SUNDAY 4 July: Red & Black cafe

Imber, Mark and I headed to the *Red & Black cafe* for dinner. Imber and I both had a Hot Chocolate US$2.50 each. Mark had the Tempeh Reuben sandwich US$6.25 with house-made tempeh/onion/mushroom rueben mix with house-made sauerkraut and Russian dressing. Imber had her favourite, *Black Dragon Noodles* US$5.

I had a great Margharetta (open) bagel with vegan cheese, tomatoes and pesto US$5. This is one of the staff member, Ryan's new dish and it's great! Unfortunately I couldn't eat it all as I'd had a hot chocolate beforehand. Why do I do this to myself? I know if I have an entree or a drink before a main meal that I'm not going to be able to eat my main meal, yet I still do this. Too many great vegan options to try I guess. Mark also had a chocolate cupcake and I got one to takeaway US$2.50 each.

US adventures part 4: week 3 in Portland & Seattle

TUESDAY 6 July: Hanging out with Mandi in Portland

Before I left for my US adventures, my friend Mandy from *Vegan Era* suggested that when I was in Portland, I should contact another Mandi from *Chic Vegan* who had just moved to the West Coast. Mandi and I sent each other a few emails before I left as well as when I had arrived in Portland and today was the day we were to meet.

I caught the bus into Portland and while I was waiting for Mandi a local African American guy tried to work his magic on me with his smooth (!) talk, designer branding on EVERY piece of his outfit, plus of course his gold and diamond accessories. Obviously didn't work at all and when he asked me for some money (!) I told him he should sell his (insert ridiculously expensive designer brand) diamond watch. He was devastated that my watch ring had fake diamonds and when Mandi arrived we tried explaining to him about the ethical issues for most diamond cultivation, but he didn't care. There are quite a lot of homeless people in Portland, but this guy was definitely not one of them. Most unusual.

Mandi and I walked around for a bit before deciding to go to *Prassad* for breakfast which is right next to a Yoga place. Mandi had already eaten so she got to watch me eat. I ordered Toast with Sprouts and Avocado US$4 which was amazing, along with the Melody Juice: greens, apple, lemon and ginger US$6. Plus I could not pass up one of their truffles: goji berries, raw chocolate, agave, cocoa nibs and cherries US$2 this was divine and I love the picture I took of the truffle – the best I've taken so far on my US adventures trip. *Prassad* has a great, relaxed, casual vibe and a healthy menu as well.

After breakfast, Mandi and I wandered around the streets of Portland and stopped at one of the local parks to do an interview. Mandi runs *Chic Vegan,* a great website full of tips and information on how to be the best ethical and fashionable vegan you can be. We got on famously and I had a great time getting to know Mandi. For lunch we headed to the vegan food carts on SW 4th and College. The cart we wanted to try was *Asaase Ital Palace.* They had just won Portland's *Vegan Iron Chef* 2010 competition that had taken place a few weeks ago, hosted by Jess from *Get Sconed!* Unfortunately for us, Qausu & Paapa were moving back home for family reasons and wouldn't be back until about 7 months time. Mandi and I fortunately had the chance to meet them as well as the new owners of the colourful cart, who would be selling meatballs ("But we'll have vegan options") hmm... Very disappointing. I had hoped to get an interview with Qausu and Paapa but this would have to wait until I returned to Brisbane and set up *Skype*.

We decided on Vegan burritos for lunch at *Fernando's Mundo Fiesta* foodcart: black beans, avocado, vegetables, rice in a wheat tortilla US$5.50. This is not a vegan food cart but it's very vegan-friendly. I also had a Banana Smoothie (meant to be Mango) from *Buddha Bites* with almond milk US$3.50.

After lunch Mandi and I headed to another vegan food cart, *Homegrown Smoker* to interview Jeff. Jeff became vegan due to his son, Jared and he was a great person to interview. Jeff ended up making us some deep-fried coconut *Oreos*, which was one of the most unusual things I've ever tasted. If deep-fried and comfort food is your thing, you'll love this food cart!

THURSDAY 8 July: Vegan Mini Mall

Today I bused it into Portland from Lake Oswego with Imber who was on her way to work. My aim for the day was to interview all the great people at the Vegan mini mall. I started the day with breakfast at *Sweetpea Baking Company* with Chad from *Food Fight!* Grocery and Brian from *Scapegoat Tattoo.* I had a poppy seed bagel with strawberry cheese US$3 and a chocolate peanut butter slice - people in the US have peanut butter in EVERYthing! - to takeaway US$3. It was a lovely day out in the hot sun.

In Australia, we've heard that the mini mall is a huge vegan shopping centre, this is not the case. No disrespect to the stores here, but four stores doesn't make a shopping centre! Obviously the power of Chinese whispers has made the mini mall out to be a LOT bigger than it is.

There are four amazing vegan stores here on SE Stark Street: *Sweetpea Baking Company, Herbivore Clothing, Food Fight!* Grocery and *Scapegoat Tattoo*. All the owners are friends who relocated here from various other areas about three or four years ago. There's really a great community vibe in Portland and this group of friends are one of the reasons for this. I headed to *Herbivore Clothing* first to do an interview with the lovely couple who run Herbivore, Michelle and Josh. They are very passionate and creative people who have a young vegan daughter, Ruby who is already a great activist. I then headed to *Scapegoat Tattoo* parlour which has an amazing gothic/retro/macabre-esque feel to it to interview Brian T Wilson who I'd loved hanging out with at the Let Live Conference a few weeks previous. Brian is a great guy with wonderful artwork who gives great bear hugs.

After that I went next door to *Food Fight!* Grocery. I hadn't been in here before. It's a great all-vegan grocery store that has just about everything vegan you can think of. I did an interview with Chad Miller who along with Josh from *Herbivore* organised the Let Live Conference that I had attended a couple of weeks ago. Chad organises a lot of vegan and activist events in Portland, which keeps him on his toes. Then I headed to *Sweetpea Baking Company* where I had wanted to interview owner Lisa Higgins, but as she wasn't in today, I ended up interviewing Ben, who I had also met at the Let Live Conference. Ben has worked with the company longer than any other job he's been in. We ended up hanging out in the sun for quite awhile – and in our interview video you can see the sun change position throughout. It was very warm. My chocolate peanut dessert thingo melted.

I headed back into Portland centre, walked around a bit more and bought some books at *Powell's* bookstore. Then headed back home to Imber and Mark's.

FRIDAY 9 July: Train travels to Seattle

Late Friday afternoon I took the *Amtrak* train from Portland to Seattle. This, I have now decided, is one of my favourite things to do in the USA. The *Amtrak* train travelled from

Portland through Vancouver, Kelso-Longview, Centralia, Olympia-Lacey, Tacoma, Kent then into Seattle. I'd never been on a train long-distance before and I thoroughly enjoyed this trip. See the Coast Starlight Route Guide on the *Amtrak* website for more information on my trip. From this moment on I have decided I need to take more scenic photos.

Rex (who I had met at the Let Live Conference in Portland, and who had offered for me to stay at his place) and his wife Rebecca picked me up from the station and we headed to *Wayward Vegan Cafe* where they had been hanging out watching punk bands as part of a fundraiser for a local sanctuary. Not my sort of music at all. Don't know the names of the bands playing, but one of them was Chad from *Food Fight!* Grocery's band. We ended up heading to a party at Derrick's place after this where there was a keg in a bar fridge and a lot of guys named... I can't remember now! This one guy entertained us for hours. How rude of me.

SATURDAY 10 July: A lot of fun in Seattle hanging out with Rex & Rebecca

Rex, Rebecca and I started off the day with breakfast at *Georgetown Liquor Company* with Anika and Kirby from *Lions Share Industries* (who I'd also met when I was in Portland for the Let Live Conference) plus a few of their friends and family. Rebecca had the Hogthrob's Sandwich US$8 and I decided to get in the spirit of things and eat something I never would have before and so I had the vegan eggs benedict: English muffin with happy ham, spinach, tomato, tofu egg, housemade hollandaise and vegan herb cream cheese spread, US$10 with some fruit on the side.

Then the gals (Rebecca, Anika and Anika's cousin, Arianne) and I went to *the Chocolate Shoebox*, a new store that sells vegan shoes and vegan chocolate - what more could one want?! I bought a few different pairs of shoes as well as a great Gourmet Vegan Fudge Sensation Bar from *Chocolate Inspirations Inc.* Rebecca picked out some shoes and bags for a *Chocolate Shoebox* photo shoot that she was doing for the store. Rebecca Bolte is a great photographer who has some of her work on show at *Wayward Vegan Cafe*.

The gals and I then headed to *Healeo* to meet Rex and Kirby who hadn't wanted to join us on our shoe expedition, but had been looking for a part for Rex's boat motor. I had a liver detox juice US$6 and we all had soft serve ice cream with a choice of topping. I chose wild blueberries US$4 YUM! *Healeo* is a great lil' juice bar, health store and soft serve place all in one.

Rebecca, Rex and I headed to the pier and Rex's boat to fix something little that ended up taking a lot longer than it was meant to. After hanging out there for awhile, speaking to some of the other boat owners and eating my divine Gourmet Vegan Fudge Sensation Bar from *Chocolate Inspirations Inc* we headed back to Des Moines where Rebecca and Rex live.

When we got home, Rebecca and I did a photo shoot in her studio for *Chocolate Shoebox* that consisted of me wearing some shoes and showing off my legs; holding a bag whilst wearing shoes and showing off my legs; as well as eating and posing with chocolate. Oh, it's a hard life I lead at times, I know. We had a great time as Rebecca loves to take photos and I love to pose! Rebecca still has a couple of other shoots with various other vegans, but the images of our shoot will be on her website or mine in the future, so keep an eye out.

Rebecca and Rex had come up with this idea of a Recipe Challenge where I would cook some sort of dish with whatever they had in their cupboards and fridge. I was up for the challenge, which ended up being Rebecca and I cooking different versions of a similar dish while Rex filmed it all. Footage will most likely be up in the Audio/Visual section of *Viva la Vegan!* or on *Vegan Threat* or one of Rex or my *YouTube* channels. The footage goes for at least 30 minutes that will have to be edited down a lot. Stay tuned I guess.

So, the Recipe Challenge meal ended up being Fried Tortillas, refried beans with a stir fry of broccoli, sweet potato, corn, capsicum (peppers) and sesame seeds sprinkled on top. Rebecca's had some sort of sauce as well as onions and tomato. Rex ended up eating a mixture of both our creations. This was great fun as part of our great day together - oh how I love these two.

After dinner, I interviewed Rebecca and Rex filmed it. Rebecca and I spoke about her transition to veganism, her photography work and a not-for-profit group *Animal Rights Education Alliance* that her and Rex run. We then recorded a podcast for Rex and Josh Harper's podcast website *Vegan Threat* which has a great lil' motto: "Threatening to make the world a better place" which doesn't sound that threatening at all really. We spoke about my many different passions: promoting veganism and health, music, my *Green Earth Festival* and much more. Josh wasn't with us so Rebecca stepped in to do the interviewing. See *Vegan Threat* for this episode soon.

I had such an amazing day with Rex and Rebecca and I'm so glad that I came to Seattle as I've been having a great time.

SUNDAY 11 July: More fun (and food) in Seattle

Rex, Rebecca and I had breakfast at *Wayward Cafe* with a couple of other lovely people: Sara and Michael. I'd met Sara's partner, Alex at the Let Live Conference and we got on really well, so it was great to meet her. Sara and Michael were going to be models for Rebecca's *Chocolate Shoebox* photo shoot as well. I really would have liked to interview both Sara (as she's a great cook) and Michael as he has a few stories to tell and works at an anti-tobacco company, but I just ran out of time.

I had the Shortstack (2) Pancakes with housemade maple syrup US$6 plus US$0.50 for banana. (Tallstack US$8 for three.) This was filling. Rebecca had the Burrito US$8. Rex had the Griddle Combo: French toast, cream cheese, tofu scramble, sausage patty and tempeh bacon US$8. *Wayward Cafe* is a great, casual place to hang out and catch up with friends.

Rebecca, Sara and Michael headed to Des Moines to do their photo shoot in Rebecca's studio, so Rex and I headed to one of Rex's favourite hangouts, in front of the Ballard Bridge over the Ship Canal at Salmon Bay. Then we went to *Healeo* for juice and to meet Kirby and Anika. Rex and I both got the Pure Simple Health juice: carrot, apple and ginger, yum, US$6. We stayed there for awhile until we went to Kirby and Anika's unit a few blocks away. I interviewed Anika about her blog on the Seattle vegan scene, *Vegan Score*, as well as Kirby and Anika's clothing company, *Lions Share Industries*. I had also interviewed Kirby previously at the Let Live Conference when I was in Portland, OR. Then Rex and I walked into the main city of Seattle for awhile and then hung out at Pier 62/63. I got to work on my tan and we chatted for ages. It was great relaxing and hanging out. Rex also filmed some footage.

Rebecca met us at the pier after her photo shoot finished and the three of us went to *Highline Vegan Bar* for lunch. We shared potato skins US$8. I had a Capanota Wrap: chunky eggplant capanota, avocado, spinach, sundried tomato cream cheez and vegan cheese curds US$7 (large US$10). Rebecca had the Caeser salad US$8 and Rex had the spinach salad US$8.

After lunch Rex, Rebecca and I went to *Sidecar*, a vegan grocery store run by volunteers with funds going to *Pigs Peace Sanctuary*, to say goodbye to Kirby & Anika. We just got there in time to say goodbye and get some group photos. After this, the three of us went around a few corners to meet Josh Harper and interview him at a local park. We walked around until we found a suitable place in Cowen Park. Rex and I had been walking around all day, myself in unsuitable-for-excessive-walking shoes, so this hurt a bit. Josh is one of the *SHAC7* group and he was imprisoned due to the *Animal Enterprise Terrorism Act* (AETA). His interview is about what lead him to being imprisoned as well as a very sad story about how his eyes were first opened to veganism. I also have another short interview with Josh I edited from the main interview where Josh speaks about the vegan scene in Seattle.

After the interview, Rex, Rebecca, Josh and I went to *Chaco Canyon* where we ordered some juice and smoothies. *Chaco Canyon* is a great organic vegetarian place near a lot of other vegan places. Rex ordered a green juice and I had a Raw Tropique: mango, bananas and apple US$5.75. I also got some takeaway to eat back in Des Moines when we were watching *Big Brother* US: Raw Green Coconut curry US$10.45, this was great. Plus a Raw Fudge Brownie: cacao with hazelnuts and dates US$4.95. This was divine.

MONDAY 12 July: Back in Portland & Papa G's

In the morning, Rex, Rebecca and I headed to the *Button Makers* store that Rex and Rebecca own and run in Georgetown. If you're into buttons (who isn't?) this is the best place for you as *Button Makers* sell as well as hire out equipment so you can make all your merchandise needs. After a quick look around, Rex dropped me off at the train station to go back to Portland. I travelled back on the *Amtrak* backwards to how I arrived. See the Coast Starlight Route Guide on Amtrak's website for more information on my trip to and from Seattle. I had an amazing weekend with Rex and Rebecca - they are now my new favourite friends!

Back in Portland with my Portland friends, Mark and Imber, who picked me up from the train station. We headed to *Papa G's* organic deli for a late lunch/early dinner. Mark had the Mac and cheeze with potato mash and vegetables US$9. Imber had the Tofu Dog: roll, tofu dog, ketchup, mustard, relish and onion US$4.50 as well as Mac & Cheeze US$4.99. I had the Organic Nachos: Kettle corn chips, taco tofu, black beans, salsa, local corn, gluten free notcho cheeze US$8.75. I also ordered an Organic Raw Avocado sandwich to have later on US$8.50 consisting of purple cabbage leaf, avocado, cucumber, shredded carrots, mixed greens and *Papa G's* cashew mayo. Mark also had a slice of their raw chocolate cake.

After lunch, Mark, Imber and I went to check out the *People's Food Co-Op* in Portland. This is a great health food style store, with bulk goods, fresh produce and a lot of vegan options. There's a great food cart right in the same area called *Sip Juice* Cart where I got a berry smoothie with rice milk, yum. Quite expensive, can't remember the price, but well worth the money.

Today Rex sent me some great video footage that he'd filmed on my last day in Seattle, encompassing hanging out at one of Rex's favourite spots in front of the Ballard Bridge over the Ship Canal at Salmon Bay, *Healeo* for fresh juice with Anika and Kirby, Pier 93 (I thought it was Pier 62/63 as it said on my photo) for sunshine appreciation, interviewing Josh Harper at Cowen Park, saying goodbye to Kirby and Anika at *Sidecar for Pigs Peace* - Yay! L-C's Seattle adventures video - LOVE it!

TUESDAY 13 July - Last night in Portland

Today was my last night in Portland. It had come quickly though sometimes not, it's weird how we experience time. Most of the past 3 weeks I had spent in Lake Oswego with my Australian vegan friend, Imber and her husband, Mark, and their two dog friends, Samba and Choco. I was glad I finally got to know Mark and spend some quality time with him. I'd only had dinner with Mark and Imber the night before their wedding about a year ago on the Sunshine Coast in Australia as well as a bit of time at the wedding, obviously. Unfortunately, Imber had started full-time work the week I arrived in Portland, so we hadn't spent that much time together. Other than my motorcycle adventure with the lovely Jackson to Mt Hood National Park and Mt Hood, as well as my Seattle adventures with my new favourite friends, I'd spent most of my time in Portland since coming to the USA.

Portland is a great town where everyone is environmentally aware, quite liberal in thinking and most people ride their bikes everywhere. Portland is one of the main vegan meccas in the USA and I'm very thankful that I had a great base when I was here as well as getting to met some wonderful Portland locals. I *will* be back.

We decided to try *Vege Thai* for dinner, which was a great idea as I love Thai food. We ordered Spring rolls to share (3 pieces) US$3.95 which were freshly made and not just the frozen ones some places serve as their own. They were delicious. I ordered the Panang curry with Tempeh US$8.50, yum. Imber ordered the Garlic Chicken US$8.50 which was also very good. Mark ordered the Pad Thai with tofu US$7.50 and black sticky rice with coconut cream US$3 and fried banana US$3.50 for dessert.

Vege Thai was a great place to dine with really friendly staff, very quick service, great food and great prices. Great spot to eat on my last night in Portland. Bye for now Mark and Imber.

US adventures part 5: Animal Rights Conference, Washington, DC

WEDNESDAY 14 July: Portland -> Washington, DC

Early this morning Mark and Imber took me to the Portland airport where I then flew to Dulles airport in Washington, DC to attend the AR Conference - one of the main reasons for my jet setting across the world. Almost 5 hours later I arrived, losing a few hours due to the time difference. At the Dulles airport they have these buses set up like trains to shuttle you from one area to the other, bizarre. I'm sure it wouldn't have taken that long to walk. I've decided Dulles is worse than LAX as I didn't think LAX was as big or as daunting as everyone makes out. I was picked up by the *Super Shuttle* bus, another of my favourite modes of transport in the USA. The bus was full as we headed to the Alexandria Mark Hotel. It took what seemed like forever to get to the hotel. A lady on the bus told me I wouldn't be able to walk to Washington from the hotel. I realised that I was actually quite a distance away from, well, pretty much anything.

I arrived at the hotel in which the staff seemed overwhelmed and everything was running late. A lovely guy holidaying with his family, including two fur friends, said he'd been waiting for his room for 4 hours! My friend, Shannon Keith who runs *ARME* and put out the documentary films *Behind the Mask* and the new *Skin Trade*, had booked a room for her, myself and two of her friends. Unfortunately due to the passing of one of Shannon's fur family members, Shannon couldn't make it to the AR Conference where *Skin Trade* was one of the film premiers and she was meant to be speaking. Since the room was booked under her name and not mine and I was using my card, this created all sorts of drama. Shannon's two other friends Gene and Ethan would be my roommates for the AR Conference. We didn't know each other at all (though I had met Ethan briefly at the Let Live Conference in Portland at the beginning of my US adventures) though we had all decided having Shannon and veganism in common was enough and were willing to give it a go.

I finally got to my room, caught up on some emails and phone calls, had a shower and went to bed. I was exhausted. The time difference from Australia -> LA hadn't really affected me, but the time difference from Portland, OR -> Washington, DC well, that was another matter.

THURSDAY 15 July: Animal Rights Conference Opening night

I was planning to go into Washington city by bus, then train from the hotel to check out some local vegan places that Saurabh from the Washington branch of the *International Vegetarian Union* had recommended the day before. However after making some calls and answering emails I went back to sleep, ever so exhausted. I ended up waking up around lunchtime, got ready and decided to have a wander around to see what was happening. Most people wouldn't be arriving until about now so I headed downstairs hoping to run into someone I knew or knew of. I met some of the *FARM* volunteers including Michael who via Cindy had offered for me to use his flatmate's acoustic/electric guitar for my performance Saturday night at the banquet. The guitar was a black *Ibanez* acoustic/electric with a heap of punk band stickers on it of bands that I'd never heard of before. I took the guitar upstairs, changed the strings and had an hour or so practice. I hadn't sung my songs or played the guitar since I'd been away from home.

I went downstairs to register for the AR Conference and after that went into the food hall where I paid US$18 for a vegan meal that wasn't that exciting at all. Hopefully I will not be doing that the whole time of the conference. I had dinner with a couple of people as well as a great guy, Michael who would end up being one of my favourite people at AR Conference. As Michael had been to all of the AR Conferences he was my go-to man for any questions and a great help all weekend. After dinner I went into the Exhibits hall to set up my *Viva la Vegan!* stall/booth/table (ever so confusing getting the US terms right) so it would all be ready for the next day. A couple of my close neighbours in the exhibit hall were from the Portland Let Live Conference. Josh from *Herbivore* and Michael & Karen Budkie from *Stop Animal Exploitation Now (SAEN)* a great group raising awareness and leading many campaigns against the vivisection industry's abuse of animals. Many people had said that Michael Budkie was a great speaker, so I looked forward to hearing him speak sometime this weekend.

When I was leaving I saw Daniel Tudor from *Sparrow Media* and spoke to him while he was setting up their table. I'd met Daniel previously in Portland, had interviewed him at the Let Live Conference and was meant to go on a road trip with him that never eventuated, so I looked forward to spending some time with him over the weekend. He ended up bunking with Gene, Ethan and I for a couple of nights as well. We had an early night this night as the next few days were sure to be full on.

FRIDAY 16 July: Animal Rights Conference

Today was a great day of meeting like minded people and a few of my *FaceBook* (and even *MySpace*) friends, including the wonderfully upbeat, positive and just an all-round great guy, Robert Cheeke from *Vegan Body Building* who has a new book out: *Vegan Bodybuilding and Fitness*. My new friend, Michael bought me some food for lunch from somewhere local (sorry can't remember the name) and I hung out with Peter Young most of the time, getting to know him and having great discussions about everything.

That night, Peter, Gene, Ethan, some other friends and I ordered some pizza from *Z Pizza* that had *Daiya* cheese and who actually delivered to the hotel in Alexandria. We spent about US$60 on vegan pizza and only got one topping - cheese! Obviously I had no say on what was ordered, boring. So we all went outside to eat and there was a guy cooking pizza in a solar oven who just so happened to be Keith McHenry, one of the founders of *Food Not Bombs*. He's a great guy and Peter had a bit of a star struck moment. Unfortunately we were way too full from our store-bought pizzas to finish Keith's solar-cooked pizzas.

The screening of *Bold Native* was on tonight and as I'd seen this great new fiction film in Portland I opted to hang out with my roomies, Gene and Ethan and get to know them better. There was a lot of action downstairs with the scheduled evening programme, around the hotel and especially in the lobby and bar area. Gene, Ethan and I went to bed earlish tonight, except for Daniel waking us up at 4:30pm to get in as well as myself doing a bit of sleep talking and scaring my roommates with my ramblings and yelling of "Where the hell am I?" This didn't wake Daniel up but freaked Gene and Ethan out a bit. I pretty much have woken myself out of a semi-conscious state each night of my US adventures saying this exact same thing, though I didn't remember saying it on this particular night.

SATURDAY 17 July: Speaking on Staging Effective Events & Performing at the Banquet

Today was my big day with my speech on *Staging Effective Events* in the afternoon and my performance at the banquet at night. I was joined by Lorri Houston from *Animal Acres* (where I had visited when I was in LA) and Alex Hershaft who was one of the main organisers of the *FARM* AR Conference. The three of us spoke at 2pm on *Staging Effective Events*. Lorri has put on many events to raise funds for *Animal Acres*, Alex has put on the AR Conference (for a number of years I believe) and myself putting on the *Green Earth Festival* - our first one was held at the Brisbane City Botanic Gardens this year and we had about 3000-4000 people in attendance.

Each of us spoke for 10 minutes each and then had about 30 minutes of questions from the audience. I am in the middle of writing a book on putting on events but it's a huge task and there's a lot of information to go into it. Keep your ears and eyes open. You can see the speech I gave and questions I answered afterwards on the *Viva la Vegan!* YouTube channel. You can also see the AR Conference website for more speeches from all of the other speakers throughout the weekend. The three of us had a great turnout to our talk, had great questions and I had wonderful feedback afterwards and throughout the rest of the weekend.

I managed to get away from my table/stall/booth for a while after my talk to practice my songs for the night. The banquet was meant to start at 6:30pm and I was to play 2 sets of 2 songs each, the first set starting at 7pm. The banquet was quite unorganised and I didn't start until after 7:30. The sound was really bad too, but I know that people aren't there to hear me perform so I did my best.

I played two songs: *My new favourite friend* which I wrote a few years ago when I was in a completely different stage of my life and also played *Good bye my love, Good bye my pain* which I released on an EP a few years ago entitled *Songs of Love, Heartbreak and Retribution* that you can download on *iTunes* or buy on *CDBaby*. This is probably my most heartbreaking song (they are my forte) as well as being most people's favourite song of mine. Normally at Animal Rights or vegan events I also perform a spoken word piece of mine, *Piece by Piece*, which is about the beginning to end of the killing floor from the eyes of the animal. It's a bit of an intense piece but necessary for the majority of people to hear.

Awards on the night went to Anthony Marr from the *Anti-Hunting Coalition* (Grassroots Activist Award), Niki Gianni (Young Activist Award) and Zoe Weil from *Institute of Humane Education* (AR Hall of Fame.) The food wasn't that exciting, and as the banquet went on we were being very silly at our table, acting as though we were in school again. In the end Peter, Gene, Ethan and I decided to take our fun outside. With most of these AR and vegan events, it's not really the specific speakers, performers or events that are actually planned for the people at the event that matter. It's the people you meet, converse with, get to know and generally develop relationships with that will hopefully be life-long. These are the best things about these events *and* my US adventures.

I ended up getting a few photos of myself with some friends. Here's some info about them.

Peter Young was definitely my favourite person at the AR Conference. We hung out most of the time together and he kept me company at my stall/booth/table as well. I must admit that I didn't really know much about Peter before my US adventures other than the fact that he'd been to prison for liberating a heap of mink. I just knew from the first time I met him in Portland that we would get on famously. The ladies definitely love Peter Young with many telling me so throughout the weekend.

Peter runs a great website *Voice of the Voiceless* that is an online tool for activists who are interested in the *Animal Liberation Front* (ALF) movement. Peter has regular updates and a mass of information on all things to do with direct action. He has Keith Mann, ALF organiser's *From Dusk til Dawn* book, and has also compiled a book on the history of ALF actions of the past 30 years, as well as an *Animal Abusers Directory* and much more.

Peter is a great speaker and speaks at many (AR) events, inspiring people to (continue to) be great activists, to get involved with eradicating the enemies of our animal friends - by hitting them where it hurts the most: their hip pocket - and being comfortable with enacting the changes that are so desperately needed even with the threat of the *Animal Enterprise Terrorism Act* (AETA) and other such threats on action and consequence.

Peter went to prison for 2 years on account of a charge of *Animal Enterprise Terrorism* after being wanted by the FBI and on the run for 7 years. Peter liberated over 8000 mink as well as foxes from various fur farms just before the pelting season in December, when every single one of the animals in fur factories in the USA get murdered. Peter gave a very inspiring statement to the court at his sentencing on 8 November 2005. See below for the statement that I found at supportpeter.com. This statement is still spoken of and oft quoted, and for obvious reasons. I hope you get something from it:

This is the customary time when the defendant expresses regret for the crimes they committed, so let me do that because I am not without my regrets. I am here today to be sentenced for my participation in releasing mink from 6 fur farms. I regret it was only 6. I'm also here today to be sentenced for my participation in the freeing of 8,000 mink from those farms. I regret it was only

8,000. It is my understanding of those 6 farms, only 2 of them have since shut down. I regret it was only 2.

More than anything, I regret my restraint, because whatever damage we did to those businesses, if those farms were left standing, and if one animal was left behind, then it wasn't enough.

I don't wish to validate this proceeding by begging for mercy or appealing to the conscience of the court, because I know if this system had a conscience I would not be here, and in my place would be all the butchers, vivisectors, and fur farmers of the world.

Just as I will remain unbowed before this court - who would see me imprisoned for an act of conscience - I will also deny the fur farmers in the room the pleasure of seeing me bow down before them. To those people here whose sheds I may have visited in 1997, let me tell you directly for the first time, it was a pleasure to raid your farms, and to free those animals you held captive. It is to those animals I answer to, not you or this court. I will forever mark those nights on your property as the most rewarding experience of my life.

And to those farmers or other savages who may read my words in the future and smile at my fate, just remember: We have put more of you in bankruptcy than you have put liberators in prison. Don't forget that.

Let me thank everyone in the courtroom who came to support me today. It is my last wish before prison that each of you drive to a nearby fur farm tonight, tear down its fence and open every cage. That's all.

It's great to meet people who are strong in their convictions, know how to get on with most people and how to read others well. Peter is a great person who is comfortable in his own skin - no matter what the gossip of the day is - who is definitely a walker and not a talker and these and more are some of the reasons why I just LOVE this guy!

My roomies Gene & Ethan were my other favourite people from the AR Conference. From just having Shannon and veganism in common to becoming firm friends, I love these guys! We had such an amazing time getting to know each other and I'm excited to hang out with them again in the future. Gene Blalock is from LA and in a band called *The Faded* whose song *Leave out the Rest* has appeared on one of the latest *Twilight* movies, which is a pretty big deal. They also appear on Shannon's latest film, *Skin Trade*. Speaking of *Skin Trade*, Gene is also the Editor and co-producer of said documentary. Due to Shannon not being able to make it to the conference, Gene did a great job of filling in for her with most of Shannon's speaking commitments. Gene is a great guy with a devious sense of humour who takes awhile to get ready, but at least you know that his hair is straightened and styled to perfection!

Ethan Wolf is from New York and a lawyer who works in child protection, you know, the horrible stuff you see on *Law & Order SVU*. He's a great guy with a quick wit and a sense of humour that some people don't get so he can sometimes come across as condescending or just sarcastic. Ethan is also the NYC contact and organiser for all things *Sea Shepherd* and he's always organising events to raise awareness or raise money for *Sea Shepherd*. As I'd now decided to go to New York after the conference, I looked forward to seeing Ethan in his hometown. Both these guys are amazing people and though quick to tease me about anything they can including talking in my sleep and the essential oil blend that I wear that just so happens to have Patchouli in it, I thank Shannon that the three of us got to be roomies. There were many other amazing people who I met at the conference who I will remain friends with - you know who you are.

Tonight was the screening of *Skin Trade* and as I'd seen it before, I sat in on one of Peter's talks with a few other activists: a round table discussion that focused on not letting fear get in the way of being active for the animals. This was the first session that I really got to participate in, as I was at my stall/table/booth most of the conference. It was quite an informative talk and great to hear so many takes on similar issues. There are many passionate people who are doing the best they see fit to help our animal friends find freedom. It's very inspiring. However, just like back home, there's always in-fighting and a bit of this happened at this talk. I'm a bit over it and I can't understand how people can't just get along. I know that maybe naive, but, WHY NOT?! After all they say there's always 3 sides of a story: one person's side, the other's and the truth, haha. I like that one.

After this Peter and I went to find one of my other favourite people at the conference, Jared Palermo who along with Linwood Bingham, had a table for Linwood's straight edge vegan clothing company, *Motive Company*. Jared's a great guy who is so charming, amicable and just a pleasure to be around. Peter, Jared and I had a lot of fun hanging out and doing silly things. The three of us hung out at the bar, met some new people and spoke to a few friends. Denis from *Bold Native* came to join us as well. Then when things were starting to slow down a bit, the wonderful Sparkle and her friends came over to cause some ruckus. Things got very weird after this, even though most of us weren't drinking. After Sparkle coloured in Jared's shoelaces and I drew some great (!) pictures with Sparkle's crayons for the guys, it was well and truly time for bed.

SUNDAY 18 July: Last day of the Animal Rights Conference

Today was the last day of the AR Conference and I got to hang out with the wonderful Robert Cheeke from *Vegan Body Building* again. Robert has a new book out, *Vegan Bodybuilding and Fitness* and he hung out with me at my stall/table/booth selling his new book, striking some bodybuilding poses - even in one of my *This is what a Vegan looks like* singlets (tank tops) - yay! It was a bit intense being in the air conditioning ALL day every day so whenever I could, I went outside to sun myself for awhile. Robert and I had a great deep and meaningful conversation (but then again, aren't they all?!) when we were sunning ourselves outside.

After sunning myself, I went over to see Will Potter from *Green is the New Red* and Josh from *Herbivore*. Will runs *Green is the New Red* a very informative site on such things as the *Animal Enterprise Terrorism Act*, *Green Scare* and has some great *Activism is not Terrorism* and *Domestic Terrorist* merchandise. I met both of these guys in Portland at the Let Live Conference and had interviewed Josh and his lovely partner, Michelle before I left Portland. *Herbivore* is one of the stores in the Vegan mini mall in Portland. Warning: Will and Josh are very silly especially when together!

I also got on really well with Karen and Michael Budkie who run *Stop Animal Exploitation Now (SAEN)* and I hope to see them in Australia soon (plus finally hear Michael speak.)

Gene, Sparkle and her friend, Ramy and his friend, Peter and I headed to *Sunflower Vegetarian Restaurant* to get some dinner for the night. It took Sparkle and I awhile to find the place and as I was meant to perform around 20:30 back at the hotel; Sparkle, Gene and I ordered some food to takeaway and drove back to the hotel.

That evening was the closing ceremony for the conference and I performed another two songs for the audience around 9pm. Saurabh from the *Veg Society of DC* gave me a great introduction but the sound was even worse than the night before. I performed *To Your Rescue* a song that I released on an EP a few years ago entitled *Songs of Love, Heartbreak and Retribution*. You can download on *iTunes* or buy on *CDBaby* as well as a new song *Not Just a Dream* that I will hopefully record properly one day soon.

This was our last night at the hotel and at the conference so we all made the most of it. I made sure I hung out and chatted with most of my new friends wherever they were before the end of the night/early morning. A mutual friend of Peter's and mine, Daphne, wanted to interview Peter so she could get him some publicity in Greece with the media contacts she has. So I filmed the interview with the two of them. I have an edited version on *YouTube* of Peter's responses to Daphne's questions.

Then I interviewed Peter in an open VIP room I had found earlier on in the night. Peter is a great person to interview and so passionate about what he believes in. That night we all met at Ramy's unit at one time or another to watch silly people get even sillier when alcohol is involved. Most of us don't even need alcohol to act silly! It was sad to know that I wouldn't be seeing my new friends for quite awhile. The amazingly dedicated and passionate, Camille Hankins from *Win Animal Rights* dropped by about 4am to say goodbye and let us hang out with Freedom, one of the beagles rescued from a laboratory that had been closed down recently. Then it was time for bed.

MONDAY 19 July: Goodbye Alexandria, Denis and I are heading to New York!

Peter and I were meant to get up to have a free breakfast (that the hotel had given my roomies and I due to a bit of a room confusion a day or so ago), maybe watch some of the talks, including Michael Budkie from *Stop Animal Exploitation Now (SAEN)*, but we ended up sleeping through the morning, checking out and then going downstairs where the conference area became quite eventful with leaflets of rumours being passed around by certain people. I won't get into it as I'm not into drama or gossip and don't surround myself with people who are, but in-fighting, bullying and disrespect within the Animal Rights and vegan communities doesn't just happen in Australia - it's international! This isn't a good thing. I don't see why we can't all get along. I know I'm naive at times and I know that I see the good in all people - even when I shouldn't - but we're all meant to be on the same page, you know, uniting to fight for those who can't fight for themselves.

My last day in Alexandria was anything but dull. I had decided due to suggestions from both Jackson as well as Mandi from *Chic Vegan*, that I would be heading to New York after the conference until I was to fly home. I was planning to either train or bus it with my new travel companion, Denis. In the end Denis hired a car as he had a bit of stock and merchandise to take with him due to the NYC *Bold Native* premiere taking place in a week's time.

Denis and I went to *Sticky Fingers Bakery* for a late lunch where we ran into Will Potter from *Green is the New Red*. I had the Hummus wrap and Denis had the Chicken Ceasar Wrap both were US$7.50 each. We also got a cupcake each and a nut brownie to takeaway, all US$2.50 each. My cupcake was Cookies and Cake. Denis had the Red Velvet cupcake. We also ran into Will Potter at the bakery.

Due to us leaving Washington, DC quite late, we got to see the sunset and watch the light retire on our Washington to New York road trip. We stopped off a couple of times to stretch our legs and I took a few scenic shots of our road trip.

Denis is a great road trip buddy. We are obsessed with a lot of the same actors (Michael Pitt!) and movies and had a great time getting to know each other. We finally arrived in New York about 10pm where we were staying at Denis' business partner, Casey's friend's place when she was out of the country. We had a great apartment on East 81st Street on the Upper East Side that would be home for a few days until my flight back to Australia.

Side note: I can't get the Alica Keys & Jay Z song *Empire State of Mind (New York)* out of my head!! 'Cause *I'm* in New York.

US adventures part 6: New York - my last week before heading Home

TUESDAY 20 July - New York with Denis

Denis and I started our day with late brunch at *Kate's Joint*, a great vegetarian place that has been open for years in the East Village. We had a very friendly server who kept us entertained and played some great 80s music, plus a security guard for Shakira or Shakira's drummer, or something. He did a bit of name-dropping. I had the multi-grain Pancakes with bananas and walnuts. Even though they were a bit burnt for my liking were yum US$6.95. Denis had the Southern fried un-Chicken cutlets US$11.95.

Then we went to visit Russell Simmon's office to see his assistant, the lovely Simone who is also vegan, a passionate activist and generally a great gal. Russell was going to be attending the premiere in NYC of *Bold Native* on Monday night. While we were there, camera crews were filming Russell's upcoming reality show that seemed pretty scripted really. Side Note: I have resigned myself to the fact that for the whole time I'm in New York, plus when I speak about New York or even think about New York, I will have the Alica Keys & Jay Z song *Empire State of Mind (New York)* in my head. I'm sorry Frank Sinatra, I just can't help it.

That night Denis and I met up with Ethan (my roomie from AR) and Andy Stepanian (one of the *SHAC7* who I'd met in Portland) at *Caravan of Dreams* for dinner. *Caravan of Dreams* is a great organic vegan place with a great atmosphere. We all shared the Non chicken Nachos US$11. Andy had the Un-chicken Ceasar Salad US$9. Denis had the Summer green pasta primevera US$17. Ethan had the Burrito monoski US$16. I had the Raw spinach quiche and a beautifully presented salad US$18 as well as a coconut shake US$6 – YUM. I wanted to wear the flower garnish in my hair, but ate it instead.

Even though the four of us were quite full, a vegan must always make room for dessert - especially when in a different city, and even more importantly when in a different country. So we went to Ethan's favourite place, *Lula's Sweet Apothecary* for dessert. I had the Classic Sundae US$6.75. FULL. We then hung out at *Altas Cafe* with a few of Andy and Ethan's friends and talked for quite a few hours until it was late and time to catch the train back home.

WEDNESDAY 21 July: More New York adventures

Denis and I headed to *Candle 79* for lunch. This is Jackson's favourite place in New York but we decided to go somewhere else due to quite expensive prices for lunch when we knew our dinner would also be expensive. I just took a photo to send to Jackson of the outside of the restaurant. We soon found out that *Candle Cafe* was just as expensive so we could have gone to either. Denis and I shared our meals, starting with the Crystal Roll US$12, then the Tuscan lasagne US$16. I had a Carrot Apple Snap juice US$4 and Denis had a Flu and Cold Fighter juice US$6. Then we shared a piece of the divine Chocolate Mousse Pie US$7, YUM. I was quite impressed with the photo I took of the pie.

Denis and I then headed to the *Metropolitan Museum of Art* where we wandered around for a few hours, though ended up getting kicked out as we'd left it too late to fully appreciate the museum. However we did see the Picasso exhibition, mediaeval exhibition (divine!) and a few others.

Denis is such a great person who I'm glad I not only met but got to hang out with - most of the time just the two of us. I can't wait to help Denis and his business partner, Casey, bring their inspiring movie, *Bold Native* to Australia.

So, Denis and I are walking along in Central park after we'd seen some series getting filmed - can't remember what it was called, bad name - and just next to me were SQUIRRELS!! By the time I'd realised this, yelled "Squirrels" and found my camera they weren't as close as they first were, so Denis and I had to stalk a few squirrels until I got some shots. The last time I saw a squirrel was when I was in Portland and I guess they're like possums. In Australia we have possums in some backyards (they delight in crawling on my roof at certain times in the night, waking me up promptly, walking across the wires to my across the road neighbours, then telling their friends it's good for them to come across and repeating this process until they get bored) or maybe koalas and kangaroos or wallabies that are in some people's backyards if big enough or if close to bushland. Anyway, I got excited about the squirrels.

Dinner tonight was at probably one of the most recommended vegan restaurants in New York, *Blossom*, a great organic, vegan place with Ethan, Nik Tyler (who I had met and interviewed in LA), his activist friend from LA, Libra Max, as well as Denis and myself. We all shared Cape Cod Cakes for an entree US$11. We decided that we'd all order an item from the menu and share the meals. I chose the Pistachio and Pepper dusted tofu US$20. Ethan chose the Lasagne US$18. Libra chose the Phyllo Roulade US$18. Nik chose the Rigatoni in Porcini cream US$18. Denis chose the Hickory basted Tempeh over Horseradish creme Fraiche US$18.

Hal, a friend of Andy's and Daniel's who I'd met at ARC, joined us just in time for dessert. Ethan had the Chocolate Ganache, which was simply DIVINE US$10. Hal and I both chose the Blossom Cheesecake, which was good but just didn't compare to the ganache US$9.

Then Nik, Denis and myself went to see *Inception* at one of the local New York cinemas with a friend of Nik's, Aaron, who was the cinematographer and producer of another film Nik is in, *Kilo*. Now, as for *Inception*. I am not a fan of these types of movies at all: too much special effects does not (in my mind) equate to a great movie due to this usually meaning a lack of quality acting, script and/or character development. But Joseph Gordon-Levitt is one of my favourite actors (see *Mysterious Skin* and *(500) Days of Summer* for proof), as is Leonardo di Caprio. I also liked Christopher Nolan's *Memento* (but couldn't stand the *Dark Knight*), so due to the positives *mostly* outweighing the bad I thought I would give it a go.

Joseph was great, Leo and his character were boring, way too much special effects that to me seems like such a waste of money. I even closed my eyes a few times. The movie had no character development or growth and you didn't really care too much about what happened to any of the characters, as you didn't really associate much with them. I like the *idea* of this movie, with the unreal vs real, dream vs reality aspect as well as the psychological scope, but it was really all over the place and way too long. But look, at least I gave it a go. Nik didn't mind it, it was Aaron's second time in two nights to see it and Denis hated it. Plus I think because we were so excited about seeing the movie it was just a bit too much of a disappointment.

THURSDAY 22 July: Last day in New York

For my last day in New York, due to me not really having been to any vegan Mexican places, Denis and I had lunch at Buritoville in Chelsea. Denis and I shared a Quesidilla. I had the Spinach Tortilla with (soy) Chicken Fahita US$7.99. Denis had the Mega Soy US$8.49.

Denis and I walked to Washington Square Park where we did an interview where Denis speaks about his film *Bold Native*, being a vegan and his upcoming projects. Then Denis went to meet a friend of his back at the apartment and I lay on the grass in the sun listening to the jazz band performing and waited for a friend David from Australia to come and meet me. David and I had both been in a music video years ago for some mutual friends of ours, Nathan & Daniel whose band at the time was Amphibious (the film clip was for *You will never be my girl*.) They are now called *Oh Tragic Vinyl Night* and I have also been in another one of their film clips: *Fast Times at BS High* where I also featured on guest vocals. Some friends and I had a film production company, *Corrugated Dolphin Productions* who filmed, produced, edited etc *Fast Times at BS High*. This was a great music video. You can see some photos from the day in the Gallery section on my leigh-chantelle.com website as well as the finished clip on *YouTube*, plus buy their song or CD on *iTunes*.

I was meant to stay with David when I was in New York, but due to him being in London the day I arrived in NYC, I decided to stay with Denis instead. David met me at the park then we walked into Soho and stopped at *Snice* for a cupcake and a smoothie. They were both amazing but I was way too full - especially considering I had a dinner date with Ethan in about an hour - not a good idea to be full so close to dinner. I hadn't hung out with an Australian for weeks and David's accent is very strong. It was a bit bizarre actually to hear the Aussie accent, but great to see him and hang out for a few hours. This was also the first time I'd hung out with a non-vegan since arriving on US soil.

David and I were going to train it to *Soy & Sake* where I was meeting Ethan for dinner, but decided to walk instead. There was some great artwork in one of the subway stations, including a mosaic piece. David then left for his home and I met Ethan for dinner.

Dinner at the Japenese restaurant, *Soy & Sake* was a great place for my last night in New York. I had Tofu Teriyaki US$4 as well as Avocado roll US$4 and Mixed Vegetable Tempura US$6. Ethan had Avocado Roll US$4, California Roll US$5, Boston Roll US$5 and Sweet Potato Tempura US$5. This was a great meal and it was a pity I couldn't eat anymore due to my afternoon tea with David before dinner.

Ethan and I headed to *Lula's Sweet Apothecary* to meet Denis and his friend, Goody-Bee then we headed back to the apartment where I packed everything up, ready for the long day ahead of me tomorrow. I had an amazing time hanging out with Denis plus loved seeing Ethan again. I need to get *Skype* when I get home so I can stay in touch with these guys and my other favourite people from the US.

FRIDAY 23 July: Thus begins the long journey back home...

I woke up at 05:00 and left Denis around 06:00 to catch a cab to take me to Penn Station. The *Amtrak* train I was meant to catch had been cancelled due to the heat - these people don't know true heat! I was re-scheduled to catch another bus later. Fortunately, the guy behind the counter was helpful and I managed to board an even earlier train than my original booking - luckily I got there early.

One of my favourite things about my US adventures was travelling by train from Portland to Seattle and back, and I had another great train trip to Washington from New York. The *Amtrak* train went from New York through Newark, Elizabeth, Trenton, Philadelphia, Wilmington, Aberdeen, Baltimore, then arrived at Washington. If you'd like to know more about my New York to Washington train trip see the Cresent route guide on the *Amtrak* website. I have always wanted to go on the *Ghan* train trip in Australia which travels from Adelaide to Alice Springs then to Darwin, so I'm definitely doing this very soon!

I arrived at Union Station where my *Super Shuttle* was early to take me to Dulles airport. *Super Shuttle* is another of my favourite ways of travel in the US. I was meant to catch a flight to LA at 15:15 but the plane was delayed and then cancelled (!!) what is happening?! I blame it on the Jupiter retrograde. So all of the people who were meant to catch the Dulles -> LAX flight had to get their tickets changed to another flight. When I went up to the counter to change my flight I was told I would have to stay overnight. I said this was not an option as I had a flight to catch home to Australia at 23:55. All sorted. I ended up changing from *United Airlines* to *American Airlines* but had to wait until 18:30 until departure.

I really like airports, but I hadn't really slept that well and was pretty exhausted right about now, as I had planned on sleeping on the flight to LA. I just had to hold off for a few hours. I rang a few friends and had great chats with people I would probably not speak to for awhile, let alone see. There was an Asian wok place so I ordered fried rice and as they cooked everything on site they made great vegan fried rice. Ate about half of the meal and would eat the rest when I arrived in LA before the long flight home. I also ate my vanilla with vanilla icing cupcake I'd bought at *Snice* yesterday in New York, so I was set for awhile. Ended up paying US$7.99 to have WiFi connection for an hour or so.

My plane finally left Washington, DC. I know we didn't have much of a chance Washington, but I'm not that impressed by you at all. I arrived in LA a bit before 22:00, finished my fried rice and talked to Peter for awhile. The flight finally left LA and I managed to sleep pretty much the whole 13 hour flight home except for when I was woken up for my breakfast and dinner.

SUNDAY 25 July: Home (Sweet?) Home

I arrived home on Sunday at 06:30 Australian time to be greeted by my parents and Cam. Don't know who was the most excited to see me, I think it was Cam. We went to *Atomica* in West End for a Veggie Breakfast (for Mum and Dad) and the Scrambled Tofu for Cam and I. Back to reality now. I unpacked my bags and a couple of boxes I'd posted home a few weeks ago. You should see my ankles and feet - they are swollen almost twice their normal size! On the plane my feet were hurting each time I put my *Vegan Wares* boots back on, but you should see them!

I hadn't watched a single Australian Football League (AFL) game since leaving about 5 weeks ago, and (sort of) looked forward to the Brisbane Lions (my team) vs Geelong Cats (my second favourite team) game. Mum had taped last night's game for me. Due to Brisbane having a horrible losing streak - don't get me started - it was a truly painful game to watch (not just for my ankles.) I didn't make it past half-time as we were losing, yet again. I decided it was time for bed at around 4pm and totally crashed for the next 15 hours. My ankles and feet were much better when I awoke, but I was still exhausted. My heart hurts from missing all the new friends I've made.

2011
July & August

My US adventures - Part One: Los Angeles, CA

Wednesday 6 July: Heading back to the US & Downtown LA

Today is the first day of my US adventures for 2011! This time I'm going for 8 weeks and I can't wait. First stop is a 13-hour flight to LA. I arrived at the airport quite early as my Dad was also flying to work this morning. So Mum dropped him off at the domestic terminal and then me at the International terminal. As I was more than 3 hours early for my flight I couldn't check in until three hours before the flight was to leave so I caught up on some computer work and emails. Had a *Subway* Vegie Delight while waiting, not the most exciting food to start my journey, but okay.

The flight left Brisbane at 10:25 and was meant to be an early arrival at LAX which ended up not happening. I pretty much fell asleep as soon as I sat in my chair, which was great as we had to wait quite awhile for people to board. I'm glad that I can fall asleep easily when flying otherwise it would be quite tedious. Luckily my ankle seems to be healed since twisting/spraining it on Saturday jumping off from the stage at Jodi's party in Byron Bay.

The 13-hour flight was good, I watched a few movies but nothing really exciting. The food on the flight consisted of penne spaghetti, 2 fruits mix, bread roll and water for lunch. Our snack a few hours later was a salad roll. Then for Breakfast just before arriving at LAX: Stir-fried vegetables, 2 fruits mix, orange juice, bread roll. *Way* too much wheat for me, it's annoying how people think that you can just serve vegans bread, bread and more bread. When I booked my tickets online I selected the option I thought was the vegan version, then I emailed customer service to double check plus confirmed when I checked in my bags. Make sure that your meal has the VGML code (*V Australia*) and you'll be fine.

I arrived in LA later than expected and removed some of my layers of clothing. I bought a SIM card at a kiosk in LAX and found the *SuperShuttle* I had booked online before leaving Brisbane. I was staying in downtown LA at my friend Denis' house. Unfortunately because of my flight being late and waiting around for more people for my *SuperShuttle* ride, I ended up not seeing Denis before him and his business partner, Casey left for Philadelphia to do some filming for their next video project - a documentary on the *SHAC7* case.

When I got to Denis' I walked around for awhile and found a Farmer's market with wonderful stone (pitted) fruits so bought a bag of them. I found a noodle place around the corner where I ordered a soba noodle dish for takeaway dinner after. Unfortunately the takeaway container was polystyrene, which is really annoying. I can't remember the last time I saw polystyrene takeaway containers used in Brisbane. Then I called some US friends, slept for a few hours, woke up to have dinner and do computer work before going to bed at midnight. The weather is beautiful in LA, looking forward to escaping Brisbane's Winter for two months.

Thursday 7 July: Adventures in Downtown LA, Baby Cakes & Shojin

I got up a few times but couldn't make myself actually get out of bed, I finally got up late around midday. I didn't sleep well due to jetlag, it's like I'm not fully present where my body is at the moment. I had my leftover noodles and fruit for breakfast and caught up on some computer work. I searched on *Happy Cow* to see where I was and worked out what places I could walk to for food. My first stop was *Tierra Cafe* for late lunch. *Tierra Cafe* is in a small food court on Wilshire Bvld with only about 3 other food vendors. Their meals are vegetarian, with a lot of vegan options, they deliver locally for lunch and are opened Monday to Friday 6:30am - 4pm. I ordered a Green Vegie Juice US$4.50 and a Vegan Taquito with more polystyrene - Mental note to self: buy one of those stainless steel containers for takeaway and leftover food - made up of oven baked taquitos, soy beef and tomatoes, topped with lettuce, soy cheese, guacamole and green enchilada sauce US$5.99.

I have also decided to start a tally for all the people who ask me for directions on my wanderings around LA/USA. I have already been asked by one lovely lass and two guys for directions to an area I've just arrived. (Score: 2) Then I headed to *Baby Cakes, a* well known shop in the vegan community overseas for having a store at *Disney World* in Florida. They also have a store in New York where they first opened. The store is my sort of style: 50s/60s inspired, girly and a lot of pink! Most of their items are gluten free and they use agave instead of sugar (in the USA not all sugar is vegan - see why on vegsource.com) with many varieties.

I ordered the chocolate coconut covered choc chip cookie US$1.75, Death by Chocolate cupcake US$4.25, mini chocolate brownie cupcake and one each of the chocolate and coconut macaroons US$1.50 each. I really want to like *Baby Cakes* as the staff are super friendly and helpful, the vibe and design is cute and kitchy inspired, but the desserts just aren't that great, okay but not great. There was some wonderful artwork I saw en route back to Denis' which made me think of my friend Adele who is a wonderful artist and designer.

I then did computer work for awhile and tried to sort out some phone issues. I had decided to go to *Shojin* for dinner, a Japanese vegan and macrobiotic restaurant that was within walking distance from Denis'. Probably in the area Denis told me not to walk by myself at night, but anyway, I left for dinner sometime after 8pm.

The staff are wonderful here, the vibe is great and the food is magnificent. I started with a Detox Elixir containing ginger, cayenne and water US$2.95 then ordered Stuffed Shitake Mushrooms: mushrooms stuffed with tofu, miso, shiso and mountain potato with soy and tempura sauce US$7.95. Dragon Roll (one of their top menu items) with shitake mushrooms and avocado with seitan and avocado on the outside, served with sweet soy sauce US$10.95. Then followed up with the Rainbow Roll (also one of their top dishes) with spicy "tuna" tofu roll inside and assorted vegetables on top US$10.95.

The photos I took of the dishes were taken with my flash on, which I prefer not to do when taking food photographs but if you want to look at other photos of their food see their website. I was mighty impressed with *Shojin* but had to takeaway half of my Rainbow Roll as I couldn't eat it all, then I was told there was dessert! Pity I had a late lunch and items from *Baby Cakes* before eating at *Shojin* as it's definitely my favourite so far in my trip. Next time I will make sure I don't eat too much that day and make up for it at dinner. I stayed up until 1am talking to my friend Brittyn from Portland, not the best plan to get over jetlag but was still great to speak to her.

Friday 8 July: Heading to Holly's & Doug's birthday

For brunch I had leftover food from the day before and fruit. I took my time in the morning with computer work and walked to Pershing Square Station to get on the train to Universal Square. While paying for my train ticket an elderly couple asked me for my help in getting seniors train tickets thus I'm changing my help-with-directions tally to my Directions & Help Tally. Score is now 3. Just so you know I'm classing a couple or a group of people as equal to 1 point.

My friend Holly picked me up at Universal Square and then we headed to *Trader Joe's,* which is similar to *WholeFoods* but less expensive as they have their own brand with a lot of their products vegan and cruelty free. I hung out with Holly last year when I was in LA and it was great to see her again and stay with her and her cat friends, Shiraz & Syra. A mutual friend of ours, Nik Tyler was hosting a party for his friend, Doug in Santa Monica with a few other friends attending. Holly and I went to *Pizza Fusion* en route to Nik's and it took us quite awhile to find the place which is hardly surprising when they had a name change to *The Pour House* (*bad* choice of name) and haven't updated the details on their website. *The Pour House* isn't vegan but they have *Daiya* cheese - which gets everyone ever so excited. I'm not really into cheese, except raw cashew cheese, so it's not that eventful for me to have food with *Daiya* cheese, but you know, when in Rome. Holly ordered a *Daiya* and spinach pizza US$7.25. Mine was a bit more exciting with a gluten free crust, *Daiya* cheese, spinach, roasted zucchini, avocado, kalamata olives and jalepenos. The basic pizza was US$7.25 + US$2 for the gluten free crust and + US$1.35 per each topping, so you do the adding, maths has never been my forte.

To celebrate Doug's birthday, we watched *Bodysong* a documentary about (I think) human life, from birth through to death set to a music score composed by *Radiohead*'s guitarist Jonny Greenwood with no dialogue. Not the sort of film I would have chosen to watch and I watch some unique films. I think it helped that most of the attendees had eaten some of (Doug's girlfriend) Emily's chocolate caramel cups that may or may not have had mind-altering substances within the mix. Emily also made a great cherry chocolate cake with carob frosting and no sugar, which sounds a lot worse than it was. It was great.

A group of us hung out after the movie and cake, walking with the dog friend that Nik regularly walks and generally hanging out. It was a great night and much later than Holly and I expected, I think we got home about 02:30.

Saturday 9 July: Dinner at Sage

A sleep in was obviously in order, so Holly and I took our time getting up and hung around Holly's flat doing our computer work. Holly is a Virtual Assistant so most of her work is done online like my Social Media Marketing. Holly is a fan of *HBO*'s *True Blood* series so she caught me up on a couple of the new episodes before the latest episode tomorrow night. We had planned dinner with some friends at Sage in *Echo Park*. I had been trying to arrange to catch up with Heather & Jenny Goldberg from *Spork Online* as I'd interviewed them last year for the launch of their online cooking courses. So when Holly and I walk into *Sage*, guess who the first person I see is? Yes, Heather who is just the cutest. We got a couple of cute photos together.

Heather and a couple of her friends joined Holly, myself, Erin and her partner Chris, Erin's friend Sarah and Justin (who I'd met last night at Nik's) for dinner. Holly and I ordered some entrees. (NOTE: in Australia we call the meal before the main course an entree, in the USA they're called starters. In the USA their main meals are called entrees. This is mighty confusing.) Polenta Galettes topped with sauteed leeks and rasin, date spread US$7.95. Succotash Fritters and Fried Heirloom tomatoes over red pepper remoulade, maple syrup and pistachio chutney US$7.50.

I had the Sriracha pasta alfredo with tri-coloured farfalle tossed in spicy alfredo with pomegranate seed, pepitas, asparagus and fresh basil US$10.50. The meal relied on garlic and a lot of spices for its flavour, as in a *lot* of garlic. I believe in the combinations of ingredients that bring their own flavours to compliment each other instead of outside flavours and rarely eat onion or garlic so this was quite intense. I can't remember what Holly had. Justin had the Stuffed Apple Ratatouille with a sweet red wine reduction, miso boiled potatoes and asparagus US$9.95. Erin ordered some sort of Mac and Cheese deep fried meal.

We all had dessert even after we were full. I got the rest of my meal for takeaway to eat tomorrow for lunch. Most of our group had the *KindKreme* ice cream - raw, organic, gourmet, vegan ice cream with three locations in LA. I chose the Brownie Sundae US$9.99 small (Large US$12.99) consisting of a raw brownie, 2 scoops of *KindKreme* IceKreme (3 scoops in the large) and raw chocolate syrup. I chose the kale, coconut and lime flavoured ice cream and the ginger and basil flavour to go with my sundae. They are unique flavour combinations but not that exciting. Justin had a white chocolate cheesecake with chocolate crust, cacao nibs, with chocolate and caramel sauce. Chris had a waffle with strawberries and ice cream. Justin took a lovely photo of myself, Erin, Holly and Sarah at the front of *Sage*.

Sunday 10 July: Scoops & Malcolm

Holly and I slept in, took our time leaving the unit and headed over to *Scoops* to have ice cream and meet the lovely Joaquin Pastor who starred as Charlie in Denis & Casey's animal liberation fictional film, *Bold Native*. Joaquin is also a very talented musician whose band, *Masxs* you should definitely check out. We all ordered the Fig & Pistachio ice cream with the *Oreo* ice cream as they were the only vegan options. Joaquin had his in a cone, Holly had chocolate sprinkles on hers. The ice cream here is great! I especially loved the pistachio and fig flavour. As I'm trying to take more photos of people instead of just food and animal photos, Holly took some cute photos of Joaquin and I.

After ice cream at *Scoops* the plan was to drop by for awhile at Gary & Keiza's place to interview Gary for *Viva La Vegan!* and to meet Malcolm the beagle who had just been rescued from a research laboratory (where animal testing takes place) by the *Beagle Freedom Project* that Shannon Keith from *ARME* is involved with. A quick visit turned into about 5 hours later as Gary and I are very similar with our viewpoints and we both can talk - who'd have thought! Gary and his partner Keiza run *Evolutus PR* providing PR for socially responsible companies. Gary also has a newish blog *The Thinking Vegan* which is mostly an abolitionist-style blog. When we were filming Gary and my interview, Malcolm kept "helping" with the direction, you know, by biting and scratching at the tripod and moving the tripod at one stage! Keiza took a lovely pic of Gary, Malcolm and I.

Holly and I ended up getting home in time for the later viewing of *True Blood* and then trying to work out how to fix an issue her computer was having. It wasn't going to happen tonight.

Monday 11 July: SunCafe & the journey to Seattle

Today Holly and I woke up early as we had a few things to do before Holly dropped me at the Burbank airport plus we had to get lunch first. We went to *SunCafe* a raw, organic restaurant in LA. Holly had a raw pesto pizza with creamy pesto, marinated mushrooms, tomato, olives, green onion and cashew cheese. Served with kale salad US$13. I ordered the Pesto Kelp noodles - raw kelp noodles with marianated vegetables smothered in creamy pesto served with kale salad US$13.

SunCafe have great food that you feel full but not bloated when you eat plus wonderful service and feel. Holly then drove me to the Burbank airport where I spoke to some friends on the phone whilst waiting for my flight to Seattle. I had a ball hanging out with Holly in LA, catching up with other friends and making some new ones. I will be back to LA for the Animal Rights conference I'm speaking at, but until then, it's off to Seattle to hang out with Rex & Rebecca.

My US adventures - Part Two: Seattle, WA

Monday 11 July: Seattle & Games Night

Rex picked me up at the Seattle/Tacoma airport after 19:00 and we headed to his and Rebecca's place in Des Moines where their vegan friends were waiting for us for Games Night to begin. Every other Monday a Games night is organised with various vegans in the Seattle community, taking place at various houses. Tonight we played *Shadows over Camelot* that I won't even attempt to explain the rules for, but it ended up being a lot easier to play than it first seemed. We all ate pizzas that Rebecca had bought and heated in the oven along with some vegetables and dips. Then we played *Scattergories*, which was a lot easier than *Shadows over Camelot*! The last time I stayed in Seattle I also stayed with Rex & Rebecca and it was probably my favourite place to be, probably a lot to do with the company.

Tuesday 12 July: Fred Myers & Button Makers

Decided to sleep in and stay home at Rex and Rebecca's to catch up on computer work until I didn't save the LA blog I was working on and lost it, grr. I was not impressed with myself so decided to walk to the local *Fred Myers* and clear my head for awhile. Oh my, now *this* was quite an experience! The store is *huge* and there is just so much stuff - everywhere - food, clothing, home ware products and more. I should have probably gone there for the first time with another vegan so they could show me what was and wasn't vegan, as I spent a lot of time reading ingredients lists of products I've never seen before. But it was fun! Organic bananas are really cheap here too - in Brisbane since the floods our bananas have been really expensive so it was great to be able to buy some bananas (organic at that) at a great price. My Directions & Help Tally score is now at 4 after another customer at the store asked if I knew where the eye drops were. Sorry, first time I've been here and all, but just so we're all clear the drops are the aisle behind where we were originally.

When Rex & Rebecca came home from work - Rex runs *Button Makers* and Rebecca is a professional photographer - I made a salad with kale, raspberries and blueberries I'd bought at *Fred Myers*, plus olives, carrots, sesame and sunflower seeds and raisins. As Rex is obsessed with vegan hotdogs, we had some of them with *Dave's Killer Bread* which is great, and watched *Big Brother* USA - a lot different than our Australian version in many ways.

Wednesday 13 July: Saltwater State Park, Thrive Café, Chocolate Shoebox & St Dames

Rex and I started the morning with a lovely stroll around Saltwater State Park where we saw some seaweed and crabs. Then we had lunch at *Thrive Cafe*. I ordered a Longevity juice with apple, beetroot, carrot and cucumber 9oz US$4. Rex ordered the amazing Buddha bowl US$11. I ordered the Oh Pastadora small US$9 with sweet tomato, Pomodoro sauce, fresh thyme, oregano and basil over raw, organic, spiralised zucchini noodles. Topped with brazil nut parmesan cheese, red bell peppers and nutritional yeast, also with Bella Burger meatballs made from sundried tomatoes, walnuts and sunflower seeds.

Rex also ordered a takeaway shake for Rebecca, the Oh My Wonka 16oz for US$7 made up of mint house-made almond milk with cacao powder, cashews, dates and pink Himilayan sea salt. They had some great raw options including a Coconut Quinoa dish and their raw cakes look amazing. After lunch Rex and I headed to the *Button Makers* store where Josh Harper who runs *Conflict Gypsy* now works. Rex and I wandered around the street and hung out at *Georgetown Records* where Rex bought some obscure LPs. I was flicking through various magazines and newspapers in the shop when I came across a local magazine called *City Arts*. I opened the magazine on a random page to find my face staring back at me with one of Rebecca's photos from the *Chocolate Shoebox* photo shoot we did last year. Bizarre but cool.

Later on Rebecca and I headed to visit *Chocolate Shoebox* where I bought a couple of shoes and owner Sadaf said that the advert would also be featured in *VegNews* magazine later in the year, so keep an eye out for that. I also found a great mostly second-hand book store where I found two astrology books. I took a photo of a few of Rebecca's framed photos of me from our shoot that are hanging up at Rex and Rebecca's place.

Rebecca and I then drove to a lovely lass Jenny's house to meet her and see the wedding cakes she makes. Rebecca does a lot of wedding photography and no-one she knows makes vegan cakes for weddings. Jenny runs *Vegan Cakes by JennyMac* and has only recently started her cake business, but with cakes such as hers I'm sure it's only a matter of time until she's well known in the Seattle community. The wedding cake she made had 3 tiers, the top tier is a gluten free spice cake, the second is vanilla cake and the bottom tier is raspberry mocha cake. The cupcakes were lemon lime with butter cream frosting and coconut garnish, plus flowers from Jenny's garden that are edible. Rebecca also took some photos. When driving to Jenny's someone asked for directions, which brings my Directions & Help Tally score to 5.

Rebecca and I also went to *Side Cart for Pigs Peace* a local all-vegan grocery store and went to a few op-shops (thrift stores) where I bought a great red and white dress and some vintage jewellery. Some of the local Animal Rights gals from Seattle were meeting at *St Dames* for dinner: Faith, Holly and Lisa plus Rebecca and I. I ordered the black bean and roasted vegetable Quesadilla US$6.75 with grilled corn tortillas, house-made sauce and cashews. Along with the Tofu Ceviche which Lisa also had US$8.25 consisting of marinated tofu, hijiki, avocado, tomato, cucumber, onions with corn tortilla chips. Rebecca ordered the mushroom risotto cakes with spicy renoulade and braised kale for US$10.25. Faith ordered the Bahn Mi Salad with greens, cilantro (coriander), red cabbage in a lemon-tahini dressing, topped with seasoned tofu, carrots, cucumber, pickled onion, jalepeno, sprout and cashews US$12.75. I also couldn't go past the Chocolate Raspberry cheesecake on an Almond and Oat crust US$6.25.

Thursday 14 July: Arya's, Side Cart, X Gym photographic exhibition & El Chupacabra

Rex and I went to brunch at a great Thai-style restaurant that has been open in Seattle for years, *Arya's* with an all-you-can-eat buffet for US$8.99 with a lot of Thai-style food including stir fried vegetables, green curry, fried rice, salads, noodles and black sticky rice with coconut cream for dessert. Then we had to go to *Side Cart* so that Rex could buy some more hot dogs (he's obsessed) before it was off to *Mighty-O Donuts* for a chocolate covered chocolate donut.

After the sugar hit Rex and I went back to *Button Makers* where I made myself useful by making some mirrored buttons for Rebecca's Art Exhibition that night - to use instead of business cards. First you cut the images out, then you place the metal, plastic and paper parts onto one side of the machine and the mirror onto the other, to make mirrored buttons.

Rebecca has recently started a website, Paunchiest.com in which she has posted an extreme workout video that Rex filmed and edited from a fitness programme at *X Gym*. Rebecca has also taken some great close up shots of some of the gym members and their muscles. Tonight was the opening night for her photographs as well as an art walk around Alki beach. Rex took a great photo of Holly from Vegan Shortcake, Rebecca and I with Rebecca's photos in the background.

Food for the night was catered by *Delicious Planet* who have a great Detox Guide. They're not vegan and spoke a bit about "happy" meats but they did make some great vegan food. A broccoli salad with pine nuts and sesame oil, Coleslaw and Mexican nut patties made from wild rice, nuts, sunflower seeds, cumin served with a mango salsa. Followed up with Holly from *Vegan Shortcake*'s raw, no GI cheesecake bites: Lemon blueberry with macadamia and almond crust and dark cherry chocolate options. I initiated a great cake display with Holly's goodies. Most unusual person and moment of the night was a pig farmer who brought by some packaging of his product: salted pig back fat, and tried to offer it to the vegans there, we were not impressed obviously. Rebecca & Rex took some great photos from the launch.

After the launch, Rex, Rebecca, Holly and I had a late dinner at *El Chupacabra* a restaurant and bar that has a lot of vegan options. Holly ordered the Veggie Tacos with rice, pinto beans, *Daiya* cheese, lettuce, onions, avocado, black olives, *Gardein* with soft white corn tortillas US$4.99. Rex ordered the Nachos consisting of corn chips with refried black beans and *Daiya* cheese, pico, olives, avocado and *Gardein* US$8.99. Rebecca ordered the Chimichanga US$7.99 Deep fried tortila filled with *Gardein*, refried black beans, rice, onions, sour cream and *Daiya* cheese. I ordered vegan Enchiladas consisting of 2 flour tortillas smothered with red enchilada sauce and *Daiya* cheese (additional US$1) plus refried black beans, *Gardein* and rice on the side US$8.99 plus guacamole additional US$1.

One of my aims for this trip is to eat more Mexican food, unfortunately they gave us the vegetarian mock meats instead of vegan for all of our meals and we had to get them all replaced. Other than that, the food was great but I think I've had a bit too much *Daiya* cheese for awhile.

Friday 15 July: Chaco Canyon, Jodee's Raw & Green Lake Park

Holly and her partner, Rick met up with Rex, Rebecca and I at *Chaco Canyon* for lunch. Rebecca had the Blue Greener blast 16oz US$5.95 with bananas, blueberries, apple juice, vegan vitamin green powder. I had the Swamp Monster juice with carrot, pear, golden beet, apple and kale small 10oz US$4.45. Rex had the Peachy Keen 10oz with peach, bananas and vanilla hemp milk US$4.95.

Holly ordered the Tempeh Bowl with tempeh, bok choy, vegetables and brown rice. I ordered the Cilantro Pesto Pizza that was raw, gluten free and soy free for US$11.95. Raw crust of sprouted buckwheat, sunflower seeds and flax seeds, topped with classic oregano sun dried tomatoes. The pizza sauce was made from house made cilantro and pumpkin seed pesto, marinated red onions and herbed ricotta with a side salad. The pizza was great. I took a photo of a great piece of artwork outside of *Chaco Canyon*.

Then Holly, Rex, Rebecca and I went to *Jodee's Raw Desserts* for some cake. Holly and I had the tiramasu US$7.25. Rex ordered the Pecan praline pie US$6.25. Rebecca ordered the frozen banana dipped in chocolate and walnuts US$3.95. Rebecca took a couple of cute photos of myself, Holly and Rex at the front of the shop being silly.

Then we went to Green Lake park where I saw SQUIRRELS! Holly's dog friend, Ani (after Ani di Franco) joined us for a walk around and Rebecca kept her entertained while I interviewed Holly and Rex filmed. I took a great photo of Ani, Holly and Rebecca and tried to get a photo of Ani by herself. How many takes do you think it takes to get a great photo of Ani? I think it was about 10. Rex made some noises to finally get the photo we were after.

For dinner we had some *Tofurky* pizzas from *Fred Myers* cut with Rex's favourite pizza cutter. Rex, Rebecca and I then watched *Big Brother* with their cat friends, Gaget and Gizmo.

Saturday 16 July: Wayward Café

Breakfast was at *Wayward Cafe* where Rex & Rebecca shared a cinnamon roll first up. Rex ordered the BBQ omelette special: fluffy omelette stuffed with BBQ soy curls, cheddar cheeze, red onion and mushrooms drizzled with ranch dressing and served with home fries US$9. Rebecca ordered the Lost Souls scramble US$8 with seasoned tofu scrambled with green peppers, onions, mushrooms, broccoli and carrots. I ordered the short stack pancakes (2 cakes) for US$6 with margarine and housemade maple syrup.

The three of us ended up heading back home and I caught up on some computer work. As we'd eaten a lot for breakfast, we had a light dinner. One of my favourite snacks this trip is organic bananas on *Dave's Killer Bread* toasted with *Earth Balance* margarine. Rebecca also made a *Gardein* chicken scalopin with Kale, zucchini, onions, green peppers and BBQ sauce.

Sunday 17 July: Plum Bistro, Healeo's, Susana, Bamboo Garden & Mercer Island

Brunch was organised at *Plum Bistro* as part of the *Seattle Breakfast Crew* who meet every Sunday at various places for vegan breakfast. Rex and Rebecca as well as Tyler and Michelle (who I'd met the other night at Games Night) both ordered the roasted garlic sweet potato fries US$5. I ordered an amazing Mexican drink, Fresh lime zest Horchata which had rice milk, pecans, lime juice and zest US$4. Rex had the Rice french toast US$11. Michelle ordered the Mayan blue corn pancakes US$13. Tyler ordered the Chocolate waffles US$10. Kyle and I ordered the Strawberry maize crepes - I don't think I've had crepes since becoming vegan over 14 years ago. They were made up of maize flour with creamy vanilla custard sauce and strawberries US$9. Rebecca had the Tres Taquitos US$6. Anika had the Quinoa nachos US$9.

After brunch we walked in the rain to *Healeo's* where I'd had soft serve ice cream last time I was in Seattle. This time I was too full. Rex and Rebecca went home and I caught up with a *FaceBook* friend, Susana (and her partner Chris) who I would be rooming with at the Animal Rights Conference in LA this weekend. We went to visit her daughter's place where she had a great vegetable garden and amazing trees out the front of her purple house.

As Susana had to work and I was waiting for Peter from *Voice of the Voiceless* to pick me up, I hung out at Susana's place in Alki where I met her dog and chicken friends and had some food made for me by Susana. Peter then picked me up and we went to *Bamboo Garden* a Chinese establishment that's been operating for quite some time in Seattle. Peter ordered the Szechwan style Fried chicken US$9.95. I ordered the Imperial style Japanese noodles with udon noodles, mock chicken and shredded vegetables US$8.95.

Then we went for an adventure to Mercer Island where Peter used to go to school and live when he was younger. I got some great scenic photos of driving from Seattle towards Mercer Island, one of the vantage points at Mercer Island looking towards Seattle, a great tree near where Peter used to live and other random Mercer Island photos.

Peter then drove me back to Rex & Rebecca's place where we had forgotten to organise to have the spare key. So at Rex's instructions, I proceeded to try to fit through the cat-flap. I thought if I can get past my hips and my breasts I'd be fine, but just after getting my hips through the cat-flap I felt a bit claustrophobic as I had my scarf and some layers on and freaked out a bit about getting stuck in there. So Peter then used his long arms to open a door from the inside and get us into the house.

Monday 18 July: Last day in Seattle

You should see my bruises from yesterday's attempting-to-climb-through-the-cat-flap mission! I also took a great photo of a slug outside Rex's place, he was sort of furry, I don't believe I've ever seen a slug like him before.

Rex and I went to the *Button Makers* store where I caught up on computer work, ate my leftover Japanese noodles from last night and waited for Peter to pick me up for my next adventure: A road trip with Peter & Sheila from Seattle to LA!

My US adventures - Part Three: Road trip from Seattle to LA

Monday 18 July: Beginning of the journey, Newport & WalMart

After hanging out at *Button Makers*, Peter picked me up to start our road trip adventure South from Seattle to LA. We then picked up a mutual friend of ours, Sheila at Greenlake, who I'd met last year at the Washington, DC Animal Rights Conference. Sheila had been staying with her Aunt and Uncle for a few nights and her Aunt made the best hummus that we ate with kale. We travelled along the I5 and stopped at *Whole Foods* in Portland to get some snacks for the trip and dinner including *Wild Wood* tofu, *Dave's Killer Bread* and banana with *Earth Balance* margarine - my favourite. Sheila and I did a bit of yoga on the grass when we had a break stop.

I am aiming to take more scenic photos on this trip. I am realising that Peter has bad music taste. He seems to be obsessed with La Bouche and *bad* 80s music. The grammar CDs he plays are interesting and obviously the conversation between the three of us is riveting, however, something needs to be done about these 80s CDs that Peter keeps playing. Sheila is encouraging this behaviour too.

That night we drove around for ages and finally decided on sleeping at Newport in a *WalMart* carpark which is what a lot of people do in America, as you are allowed to park there without getting moved on. It was freezing around 4am when Sheila and I went to the bathroom. It's meant to be summer over here and at this moment I'm not impressed with the weather.

Tuesday 19 July: Newport beach, Coos Bays, Brandon Marsh, Battle Rock & Cresent City with Robert

The weather is still not that accommodating. It's overcast but at least it's not raining. We stopped at a coffee shop to get some coffee for Peter and Sheila and then we walked along the quaint, little streets where we saw cute signs. We walked along the beach where the water was freezing and the sand so dirty. Peter said it's due to the rain and the sand would normally be cleaner, I don't believe this. We have beautiful white sand and blue seas in Australia.

I had a shower at the local Newport pool while Peter and Sheila used the WIFI outside and then we went *Oceania Natural Foods Co-Op* a great health food store with a cold salad bar and hot food bar. I had a bowl with brown rice, olives, tempeh chicken salad and the other vegan salad options US$4.75. I *love* the photo I took of my meal. Sheila had something similar. Peter had carrots, hummus, dips and apples. I also had a chocolate cookie and took an amazing photo when the cookie was in the paper bag. Hope you get as excited as I do when I take a great food photo.

I took various photos of our drive through Oregon. There is a lot of 80s music I love, for example: Stevie Nicks, Lindsey Buckingham, Kate Bush, Prince, Heart, Gloria Estefan, Tom Petty, Michael Jackson, Janet Jackson, Taylor Dayne, Rick Astley etc plus many other great one hit wonder songs, *none* of which were featured in any of the horrible 80s compilations Peter plays in the car. Just saying.

In Coos Bays I saw a picture of the *Ghostbusters* logo on a store that also had a sign saying it was a paranormal shop. We couldn't pass by this. So we went into the *PSI of Oregon* shop that specialise in paranormal research and they had a few great stories to share with us including many a ghost sighting plus when to tell if a ghost is real or fake. I bought a great Road Atlas for US$1 from the store and then we passed on through to a lighthouse opposite Brandon Marsh. It was a lovely place and I took some photos of Peter and Sheila on the beach. There was this great lil' beach shack on the beach. It's made up of a heap of different pieces of washed up wood that aren't stuck or held together in anyway. It was really cool. I also took a pic of a lovely seagull who let me come up really close to him to take a photo. Poser.

I am not allowed to drive as Peter is scared that due to the fact in Australia we drive on the *right* side of the road (being the left) and our cars have the steering wheel on the right side of the car, I would cause some sort of accident. Whatever.

Then we decided not to drive past an amazing view along the coast, called Battle Rock due to a two week battle between the native Indians and the white settlers when the white people claimed the land without any okay from the Indians. For such a horrible story and history, it's such a beautiful place. The view was wonderful and I took some great photos of flowers, seaweed, rocks and caves.

Sheila, Peter and I walked up to the top of the rock and could see over to where we parked. After our big hike up and down the large rock, we finished our road trip for the night when we met up with Robert Cheeke from *Vegan Bodybuilding* at a motel in Cresent City. Robert was heading up North when we were heading South and we had planned to catch up somewhere on the road. As he'd just had a cheque from book sales of his book *Vegan Bodybuilding & Fitness*, Robert paid for the four of us to stay in the motel that night. We went to the local supermarket to buy a few things for dinner including *Gardein* Tuscan "chicken" breasts, *Wild Wood* tofu, kale, Pico de Gallo: onion, tomato, coriander; avocado, tortillas and Sheila's Aunty's hummus for dinner. I made "chicken" and tofu tortillas for the four of us for dinner. They were yum. We went to bed quite early.

Wednesday 20 July: Haircuts from Sheila, Klamath River, Whales, Elk, Arcata, Humbolt Redwoods State Park & Lost Hills

Before we left the motel - due to Peter harassing Sheila about cutting his hair (which looked fine), Robert wanting a haircut and me needing a bit of a clean up of the back of my hair where I may or may not have a mullet - Sheila brought out her scissors and clippers and did her thang. Then we hit the road and picked up a hitchhiker named Douglas who was on his way to Arcata where we were heading.

Along the way we crossed over Klamath River where there were a heap of people all along the bridge taking photos and looking at something in the water. We crossed the bridge and I asked one of the truck drivers what was so exciting. He said I'd not believe it if he told me and I said try me. He said that there was a mother whale and her baby who were hanging out in the area for about a month, today they were swimming underneath the bridge. So cute. So we walked over to the bridge and followed the whales from side to side. I'm sure the whales were having quite a time seeing how many times all the silly humans would follow them to one side of the bridge just to follow them back to the other!

Then there was a sign for an elk area so we drove there and I got some great photos of the elk hanging out. I may or may not have been allowed to go as close as I did to the elk, but the pics I got were good. Douglas the hitchhiker took some good photos of Peter, Sheila and I on top of our rental car.

We arrived in Arcata - which has a similar vibe to the Byron Bay/Lismore area in Northern New South Wales back home in Australia. We dropped Douglas off and went to their *Co-Op* where we had some lunch. I bought some burritos and a mini pumpkin pie US$4.75 which I thought was savoury, but it ended up being sweet. Unlike in Australia, it seems pies are really only eaten in the US for dessert and especially for Thanksgiving. You live and learn.

Then we made our way to Humboldt Redwoods State Park where people camp and there are walking tracks. We got out of the car and wandered around the park checking out the trees and following one of the walking trails. I took some really great photos of the trees, Sheila and Peter. Sheila took a great photo of me lying down on the grass.

We'd heard of a tree that you can drive a car through, so we headed to Leggett where I finally got to drive the car - just through the tree a few times when Sheila and Peter were on the roof - but it's still my first time driving a car in the US. The tree is 2400 years old, with a height of 315ft (approx 96m) and a 21ft (approx 6.5m) diameter - it was pretty impressive.

We all had such an amazing day with whales and elk and trees - oh my! We stayed the night at a truck stop in Lost Hills in the middle of the desert very close to Los Angeles where we would be tomorrow for the Animal Rights conference. We saw rabbits and squirrels and the weather was great.

Thursday 21 July: Lost Hills to Westin LAX

The sun woke me up and I tried to get some more sleep outside on the sleeping bag moving with the shade of the car as the sun moved. After awhile the Sun got a bit too much for the three of us and we ended up leaving Lost Hills. On the way out of the truck stop there were a couple of squirrels catching some shade from a sign on the side of a fence, they were spread out trying to keep cool, but were too quick for me to get a photo. Cutest.

After our wonderful road trip along the coast road with great scenery and exciting places to stop along the way, the way into LA was just stretches of different types of farms as well as concrete when we got closer. The three of us stopped off just before LA for Peter to do some photocopying and I caught up on some computer work.

We arrived at the Westin LAX Hotel just before 16:00 (as Peter had promised) for registration at the Animal Rights Conference. The three of us had such an amazing time on our road trip, thanks Peter & Sheila. Our next adventures are the AR Conference in LA.

My US adventures - Part Four: Animal Rights Conference LA

Thursday 21 July: Arrival, Vegucated & Veggie Grill

Peter kept to his word by making sure we arrived at the AR Conference at the Westin LAX Hotel by 16:00. I caught up with my roomies: Brittyn from Portland and Susana from Seattle who went downstairs to register while Peter, Sheila and I showered.

One of the things I was excited about was to finally meet Marisa Miller Wolfson whose new documentary, *Vegucated* screened at 5pm. The documentary is a fun, happily contagious (like Marissa) adventure about three New Yorkers who go vegan for six weeks and the effects this change has on their lives. Marissa said in the opening that the beginning to end of the film were all done with low budget. This is noticeable in some parts, but overall the film is great and it will be launched all over the country soon.

I finally caught up with Denis and his mum, Anne who were also in the audience and spent a bit of time with the two of them before they had to leave and I had to eat. For dinner Sarah from *Xs to Os Bakery* organised takeaway from *Veggie Grill* where I had the Bali Bliss US$6.75: Indonesian styled tempeh, sautéed and grilled with lettuce, tomato, red onion, chipotle ranch on a bed of kale. I had dinner with Sarah, her partner Linwood from *Motive Clothing Company* and good friend Jared near the Motive table. I look forward to getting to know Sarah and Lin better. I already miss hanging out with Peter and Sheila.

Friday 22 July: Panels, Intersection & Ramy's Room

Today I slept in, did my washing from the road trip and finished my Seattle blog. I met Susana and Brittyn at the hotel restaurant for lunch which was about US$20 for sandwiches, a wild rice dish, salad, biscuits and carrot cake. The carrot cake was good, the rest, not so. The three of us sat down with a friend from last year's conference, Keith McHenry from *Food not Bombs*. Keith said he's getting too old for prison now as he caught us up on his latest prison story. Another great thing about the conference, is wherever you walk, you will see someone you know. One of the people was Brian Vincent from *Stop UBC Animal Research*. He always dresses well.

At 14:00 I attended the seminar on *Marketing Our Message* - Improving effectiveness of advocacy through research to see a FaceBook friend of mine, Carol Glasser speak. Carol is friends with many of my friends and runs a really informative feminist and Animal Rights blog, *Vegina*. Carol was joined by Nick Cooney, who had released a book: *Change of Heart: What Psychology can teach us about spreading Social Change.* Carol is a wonderful speaker and really passionate. I have a feeling we will get on well. I learned a lot from their speeches including how to not let your own assumptions of what is important - or what you think others believe is important - stop you from understanding exactly what is important to others. Nick gave a great example of how when people were faced with 4 different options of promoting environmentalism, one was a save-money-focused tactic, another was more of an "everyone else is doing this, why aren't you?" and two others. I assumed that the saving money option would be the most effective, however it was the following of the masses that worked the best. Food for thought. I have to buy Nick's book plus Will Potter's *Green is the New Red* book whilst here.

Straight after that I went to see Peter from *Voice of the Voiceless* talk about Applying Direct Action: Getting attention and changing behaviour through direct economic & social pressure with the always inspiring ladies: Camille Hankins from *WAR - Win Animal Rights* and Shannon Keith from *ARME* who I finally met in person. Friends Nik and Ramy dropped by to instil some silliness into my night. The three of us ended up at the *SAEN: Stop Animal Exploitation Now* casual meet and greet plus dinner, along with Peter, Jared, Sheila, Brittyn, Susana, Lin and Sarah where we found out some information about *SAEN* and had free dinner from *Veggie Grill*. There were many things happening with an evening plenary where Peter and I stopped by just in time to hear Will Potter talk as part of the panel on activist repression.

At 22:00 I went upstairs to an informal gathering and discussion organised by Carol from *Vegina* and her like-minded friend and partner-in-protests, Nicoal Renee Sheen from *Band of Mercy*. These two ladies are inspiring with the way they articulate the sometimes hard-hitting issues that need to be raised in our movement including the link between animal liberation and feminism - two of my favourite things as well. Carol has uploaded a pamphlet that her and Nicoal have written together on her *Vegina* blog.

I believe that everything I am interested in is related to each other: veganism, animal rights, feminism, human rights, environmentalism, social justice, third world and hunger issues. I don't understand how some people don't see how these all link. A friend once asked me if a mutual friend of ours was really vegan due to the fact that he consumed a particularly well-known brand of soft drink/soda and that he bought items of clothing new from a certain well-known department stores that were made in China. I said that it didn't make him not vegan and that just as all vegans have different reasons to why they became vegan, they also have different passions and choose what other things to also be passionate about. I understand it can be overwhelming as it's hard to unsee and unknow something once you've seen it... This is probably another totally separate blog for a later date me thinks.

After being intellectually stimulated by the ladies and witnessing great participation from other like-minded folks, I headed to Ramy's room where the rest of the group had ended up to be entertained in other ways.

Saturday 23 July: Interviews, my Promoting on the Internet talk, Native Foods & the Helipad

Susana and Brittyn get up early for breakfast in the mornings and bring me a bagel each day for later on when I get out of bed. A negative thing about the conference when it's located in large hotels is that the food isn't that great. A few people have mentioned something about the unions and how outside food vendors aren't allowed to cook and/or sell their food in the hotel anymore. I think this can be worked around somehow. I got a bit of computer work done, ate my bagel and headed downstairs. I met a lovely rescue wolf.

Gary and Kezia from *Evolotus PR* who I hung out with in LA, dropped by and they interviewed me for their blog *The Thinking Vegan*. Carol, who is now my new favourite friend, bought me a *Veggie Grill* chicken Ceasar wrap with a quinoa salad for lunch. After lunch Gary and Kezia interviewed Carol for *the Thinking Vegan* and then I interviewed Carol.

At 17:00 I was part of the panel speaking about *Promoting on the Internet:* websites, e-newsletters, blogs, *FaceBook, Twitter, YouTube*. I was joined by the wonderful Jasmine Singer from *Our Hen House,* and Andrew Kirschner who is a candidate for *the Humane Party:* a political party committed to the rights of all animals. Susana took some pics of our talk.

It was great to see the room packed and so many friendly faces: Holly and Nik, Peter, Gary and Kezia, Brittyn and Susana, Carol, and many more - you know who you are. You can see the *Viva la Vegan! YouTube* channel for the video of my talk on *Twitter* and Social Media Marketing.

Susana also took photos of the three of us after our panel had ended, plus many people came up to ask questions/tell us how great we were ;) Dina came up to see me, she was one of a handful of people who saw my talk on *Staging Effective Events* last year with Alex Hershaft from *FARM* and Lori Houston from *Animal Acres*. Eric from *Happy Cow* also came up to say hi. Was great to meet him and hopefully we'll catch up before I leave LA.

After our talk most people were heading to the banquet that I had decided not to go to this year. I ended up interviewing Shaun Monson from *Earthlings* instead. I can't wait for his new film *Unity*. Then I hung out with Nik & Holly and we took some photos.

Sarah and Lin organised *Native Foods* takeaway for dinner, so Holly and I headed to their room to eat our dinner together. Holly had the Spring Kale Salad: raw crunchy kale, shredded cabbage, apple and avocado tossed with maple orange dressing, topped with currants, almonds and creamy tahini drizzle US$8.95. I had the Sweet Potato Taquitos - crispy corn tortillas filled with coconut mashed sweet potatoes, drizzled with Native Chipolte crema and served with guacamole US$6.95. I also followed that up with Cheesecake - rich cream cheese filling, ginger granola crust, served with blueberries.

After dinner we found Karla who I'd met at last year's ARC and her work partner, Scotlund who runs *Animal Rescue Corps*. I did an interview with Scotlund back in our room. It was about this time when the banquet was over, so Holly and I went downstairs to see who was out and about. We ran into Sparkle from *The Only Sparkle* and Robyn who runs *Open the Cages Alliance* with her partner Adam and got Brian to take a photo of the four of us.

Then we went down around the bar area, which isn't that exciting when you don't drink, but it was good to catch up with people including Jasmine and her partner Mariann from *Our Hen House*. As well as Gene from band *The Faded* who was my roomie last year, always great to see him.

There was so much happening at the hotel this night. Ramy was having a few people in his room including Holly, Nik and Alicia. Friend Mike from Portland was performing Woody Guthrie-inspired political acoustic tunes under his moniker *Mike XVX* and various other people who I wanted to catch up with were doing various other things. It was a night of seeing a few people here and there before moving to the next group.

Peter has been carrying on for over a year about a supposedly secret rooftop hot tub (spa) that I don't believe actually exists - I think it's just a line he uses. Last year in Washington DC Peter, Jared and myself had gone looking for said hot tub that we didn't find which forced Peter to come to the conclusion that the hot tub was actually really in LA. Cut to now. Peter and I go looking for this (probably made up) hot tub. We explored each corner of the top floor and found the space that *could* have had a hot tub there at *some* stage. Peter was devastated and heartbroken that this was the end of his "let's find the hot tub" story though I can vouch for the fact that there were water pipes in a certain area leading me to believe that there actually *was* a hot tub/spa there at some stage. Hmm.

To get Peter out of his slump that the hot tub was no longer in existence, I decided that we needed to find something better. To which I found a landing pad/helicopter landing pad. Pretty impressive, the views were breathtaking. Peter was meant to take a photo of me spinning around in the middle of the red circle of the landing in my red dress, but didn't. Would have been a great photo but the lighting wasn't that good anyway. Being up on the roof reminds me of one of my favourite singer/songwriters, Kate Bush's songs *Top of the City* from my favourite album of hers, *The Red Shoes*. Make sure you read the lyrics. If you enjoy reading biographies, I strongly suggest you read *Under the Ivy*. It was beautiful up on the roof. Take me up to the top of the city, Peter.

Sunday 24 July: Interviews, last day of the conference and sleeping on top of the City

After catching up on computer work, my focus for the day was to get as many interviews as I could with friends and other vegan activists who inspire me and hopefully will inspire others. First up I saw Justin and Peter in the lobby, and since we had all managed to dress in white to match each other today, we had a photo taken together. A lot of people say that Justin and Peter look like brothers. They have a few mannerisms that are similar and are both tall with glasses. Hmm.

My first interview for the day was with Nathan Runkle from *Mercy for Animals* who are probably my favourite Animal Rights organisation. Nathan became vegan after reading a vegan pamphlet, started *Mercy for Animals*, has educated so many of the mainstream public to the horrors of animal agriculture and their latest success story is that of the *Farm to Fridge* tour where the group tour around certain parts of the USA showing the undercover footage of where food really comes from.

Next I interviewed Nick Cooney from the *Humane League*. Then I interviewed Sarah Preston who runs *Xs to Os Bakery* in Troy, NY and Sarah's partner, Linwood Bingham who runs *Motive Clothing*. Then I interviewed Jared who is working on a new online video series, *Alternative Explorers*. Jared's coming to visit me back home in Brisbane in September so that will be fun.

A few people had mentioned another Australian gal, Shelley who was also at the conference. We finally met, and had a photo taken of Shelley, my roomie Susana from Seattle and I. I then interviewed Shelley who has an extremely successful *YouTube* channel. Next up, I thoroughly enjoyed my interview with Holly's friend, Heather who runs a holistic health website *Live Natural, Live Well*.

At 17:00 Peter was speaking about *Coping With Activist Repression: Dealing with enforcement, permits, arrests, documenting, doing prison time* along with Camille Hankins from *Win Animal Rights*, Dara Lovitz who wrote *Muzzling the Movement* and Dave Simon from *Animal Protection & Rescue League*. Peter runs a website, *Voice of the Voiceless* and releases various ALF books. He is always great to see speak, as is Camille.

After the talk all the tables were getting packed up by all the exhibitors. I interviewed Will Potter who runs a great informative website, *Green is the new Red* and has just released a book with the same name. I always enjoy hanging out with Will and look forward to catching up with his gal, Ashley when I'm in New York. After my interview with Will, I headed back downstairs to help Keith pack up the *Food not Bombs* table and then we had an interview. Keith is really inspiring and I always learn a lot speaking to him. I also interviewed Bryan Monell but the video camera stopped before we had finished properly. Bryan wasn't too happy with his responses, which is too bad as it would have been great for you to see. Bryan is an amazing activist who has done so many undercover investigations and still manages to keep a smile on his face.

Ramy was meant to have a party at his place and as his parties are always fun, silly and debaucherous we were all looking forward to it. However him and his gal decided to drive hours away for dinner and we weren't able to contact them until the early hours of the morning. Gene and Sparkle went to *Veggie Grill* to get takeaway food for us, Peter, Brittyn and Susana. I had the Grillin' Chickin' US$8.95: Grilled chillin' chickin', avocado, lettuce, tomato, red onion, cilantro pesto, Chipotle ranch on a wheat roll.

Due to no party at Ramy's and most people being exhausted from a big weekend and late nights, most people hung around the bar and the bar area until the early hours of the morning. It was pretty late when Peter and I went back to the landing pad on the top of the hotel to sleep there the night. What wonderful views we had. West Century Blvd looked so quiet. At about 6am it got too cold for me, so I headed back to my warm bed, but not before taking a few photos of course.

Monday 25 July: End of the Animal Rights conference

My roomies, Brittyn and Susana left to go back home to Portland and Seattle (respectively) and I caught up on some computer work, showed Sparkle how to tie bows in her hair and spent some time with Sparkle and Peter before leaving. The three of us took some great photos of each other.

Overall, the LA Animal Rights Conference was a great event with many people from various states in the USA and beyond. I thoroughly enjoyed hanging out with friends, making new ones and networking and was quite impressed with the amount of interviews I had with people! Thanks to everyone from *FARM* who put in the time and energy to make this year another educational and fun event! Until next time...

My US adventures 2011 - Part Five: Los Angeles II

Monday 25 July: Native Foods, Karaoke & Denis'

After my AR Conference adventures, Peter from *Voice of the Voiceless* and I left the hotel, and went to *Native Foods* for lunch. Peter had the Chilli Cheese Fries: seasoned potato fries smothered in homemade Native Chilli, topped with Native Cheese and diced red onions US$ 5.95. I took a great photo of Peter with the fries as he wanted to "be in my blog." Cutest. I had the Greek Gyro: thinly sliced Native Peppered Seitan sautéed with shallots on quinoa, steamed vegetables, and kale with lemon garlic sauce and hummus. Served with grilled flatbread US$9.95. I also had their Lavender Lemonade and a Chocolate Love Pie: thick and lustfully (!) creamy chocolate filling in a delicious spiced almond crust US$2.95 to takeaway.

Then we went to *Whole Foods* to buy some snacks, headed back to the hotel to pick up Sheila after her and a lot of others had attended the *UCLA* demo organised by *SAEN*. The three of us then drove towards Denis' place in downtown LA to go to karaoke with Jasmin and Mariann from *Our Hen House* and some other friends.

Karaoke took place underneath my favourite restaurant in LA: *Shojin* near a games arcade. Peter showed Sheila and I how to play *Pac-Man* correctly at the arcade and then we went to meet everyone to sing karaoke! Now, I love karaoke and I love singing. Years ago my friend from school Michelle and I would go to karaoke most Friday nights. Shelley would pick me up from the music store I managed at Indooroopilly, we'd get takeaway noodles and alcohol (not that I condone this behaviour now) head over to my sister, Lou's place with her housemate, Carla, get ready and then join the others who would sing karaoke. Shell would never sing, she'd just watch me. My favourite karaoke song is *Stop Dragging My Heart Around* by Stevie Nicks and Tom Petty. I did karaoke every Friday night for ages.

Karaoke is a great time for me to pretend I'm Stevie Nicks, so I love it! Not only were Jasmin and Mariann there, but also Nathan from *Mercy for Animals*, Jackie from *Alternative Outfitters*, Mikko and Ari, Justin, some of Ari's friends along with Sheila, Peter and I. Jasmin, Ari and Sheila sang a heap of show tunes and musical numbers, I sang a few Fleetwood Mac and Stevie

Nicks songs, plus Tracy Chapman's classic *Fast Car* with Ari and Jasmin, and my fave Vanessa Carlton song, *White Houses* (Lindsey Buckingham plays guitar on this song!) that I have only seen in one other karaoke place. Justin took some great photos from our karaoke night.

Denis and Andy ended up coming along later as they'd been filming some scenes for the latest SHAQ7 documentary that Denis and his business partner, Casey are working on. Peter had gotten over his stage fright when Denis and Andy arrived and he had started to warm up and was willing to sing. I think *Go Your Own Way* was sung by Peter, Sheila and I.

I *love* the photo Justin took of Sheila, Peter, Denis and I! I love this photo because Sheila and Peter are engrossed in singing Hillary Duff, I'm just, you know, posing, and Denis' face shows that he's unsure of what exactly he has joined. Such a fun time. When Justin first sent me his photos from Vegan Karaoke I laughed SO much at the photo I just described. Sheila and Peter were singing the Hillary Duff song *The Beat of my Heart*. They also unfortunately sung La Bouche's *Sweet Dreams* and Bananarama's *Cruel Summer*. I hope you feel for me sharing the car with these two on our road trip from Seattle to LA.

I also did Heart's *Alone* where I impressed myself with getting all the high notes. The night ended up being quite expensive and I think we were there for about 6 hours! We ended up heading back to Denis' where Sheila, Peter and I hung out with Justin, Christina and Hal, Andy and Denis until I went to sleep - tomorrow would be an early morning. I took some really cute pics of Denis and Sheila with Denis' dog friend, Zelda.

Tuesday 26 July: Santa Monica, Euphoria Loves Rawvolution, Our Hen House Pot Luck & back to Holly's

Very early in the morning, Peter and I dropped Sheila off at the airport and then we drove to Santa Monica where Peter dropped me off so I could catch up with Eric from *Happy Cow* who I had met at the AR Conference a few days ago at my talk about Promoting on the Internet. Eric's wife, Diana made me some banana and nut butter muffins with blueberries and strawberries for breakfast. Eric and I talked shop for awhile before walking to the Santa Monica promenade and then walking back along the beach. On the walk back I met a SQUIRREL! I got some cute photos. What a poser.

Eric and I both caught up on some computer work before walking to lunch at *Euphoria Loves Rawvolution* where we shared the Red Endhilada $US12.50: chili ancho wrap with oregano cashew cheese, mango salsa on a bed of romaine. I also had an amazing Mango Smoothie. Eric and I also shared the Indonesia Noodle Affair US$11.50: kelp noodles in cashew coconut chilli sauce topped with garlic paprika drizzle, nori and red bell peppers. These meals are both Eric's favourites and they were a great choice.

After lunch, Eric and I walked back to Eric's and did a bit more computer work before Denis picked me up to go to his office and get ready for the *Our Hen House* pot luck party. Before the party, we set up tables and chairs. I also helped Denis film an interview with Carol Glasser from *Vegina*. The interview is trying to raise awareness to a court case Carol and some other activists are involved in against the UCLA Police.

Most of my friends in the US live in LA so I always like to attend events in LA as I'm always going to know a heap of people - and if by chance I don't, I will by the end of the night! Jasmin and Mariann organised a potluck to celebrate them being in LA. There was SO much food, I couldn't eat everything, but I did try. It was a great night, with great people and great food. Justin took some photos for me: with Erin who has a photography business called Pixie Portraits; with Andy, with Cameron who takes amazing photos on his Yogatography website; one with Alicia and one of my favourite photos with Kezia, myself, Gary and Heather. Gary and Kezia run *Evolotus PR* company and Heather runs *Live Natural, Live Well*. I have interviews with both Gary and Heather on my *YouTube* channel.

After a great night, I said goodbye to Peter as he was heading off on the road again and said goodbye to my other LA friends. I don't plan on coming back to the US next year, but that's what I said last year. Then I went back to Holly's to hang out with her and her cat friends for a few days.

Wednesday 27 July: Café Gratitude, Nik on TV & True Blood

Kezia and Gary took me to *Cafe Gratitude* for lunch where I ran into an Australian vegan living in LA, Andrew Gunsberg (also known as Andrew G when he hosted our *Australian Idol*). Andrew and I have a heap of friends in common and have been email and *FaceBook* friends for years. Andrew had one of my first *Viva la Vegan!* Recipe Calendars (now recycled recipe cards) back in 2006 but we've never actually met before. So it was quite bizarre to run into him at a restaurant in LA. Andrew now lives in LA with his beautiful wife, hosts Paula Abdul's *Live to Dance* plus continues to host the *Hot Hits in LA* live from LA to Australia each Saturday night. One of his friends took a cute photo of us.

I started with the I am Luscious smoothie US$8 Almond milk, fig, date, raw cacao and vanilla bean smoothie. I also had the I am Nourished live sandwich US$13 with almond pate, seasonal vegetables, avocado and mustard sauce on live curry bread. Gary had the I am Knowing live nachos US$12 with cooked black beans, guacomole, salsa fresca, nacho cheese and homemade crackers. Kezia had the I am Extraordinary BLT sandwich US$11 with sautéed maple coconut, romaine lettuce, sliced tomato and avocado, served with chipotle aioli on toasted Panini bread.

Then we had to have dessert, as they looked amazing. Gary had the I am Super Dark Chocolate Nugget US$3.50 an intense, bittersweet nugget of ground cacao nibs, almond butter & maca, minimally sweetened with low-glycemic yacon. Kezia had the I am Magnificent Chocolate Mousse US$8 A light, smooth and creamy raw cacao mousse. I had the Raspberry Chocolate Layer Cake that matched my pink dress really well - it is all about accessorising after all. The waitress who is also a photographer took a great photo of the three of us together.

Then we went to *Wholefoods* to try to find some vegan product for my hair. I shaved my head in March and I've never had it this short, so I'm not sure exactly what to do with it. We didn't find any good hair products, though Kezia and Gary gave me a good vegan tour of the store. They dropped me back home to Holly's where I caught up on some computer work before Holly got home. That night Holly and I were excited to watch our actor friend, Nik Tyler on TV. He was starring as a photographer on the *Joey and Melissa show*, a family friendly show that is not very funny with a lot of canned laughter, but it was still exciting to see Nik on TV! Then Holly caught me up on the *True Blood* episodes I had missed and we stayed up too late chatting. Love this gal.

Thursday 28 July: Alternative Outfitters, Clara's Cakes & M Café de Chaya

Holly and I met Jackie from *Alternative Outfitters* at her store in Pasadena where Jackie sells vegan shoes, bags, accessories, makeup, clothes and more. I did an interview with Jackie and bought some goodies. Then we caught up with the young and inspiring vegan baker, Clara who has a cupcake business, *Clara's Cakes* that she runs when she's not at school, as well as her blog *Clara in Veganland*. I interviewed Clara and we took some photos.

Then Holly and I went to *M Cafe de Chaya* at Melrose for a late lunch/early dinner. I had the 3 signature salad combination for US$9.75 Beetroot Quinoa, Kale with Spicy Peanut Dressing, Sesame Soba Noodle Salad. As well as the Shiitake-Avocado Roll (2 pieces) $2.25 sweet soy-glazed shiitake, avocado, cucumber, & toasted sesame seed; plus the Garden Hand Roll US$2.25 avocado, cucumber, chives, carrot, braised tofu, umeboshi paste with fresh shiso leaficy. I love the photo I took of this. Holly had the The California Club sandwich US$11.25 a triple-decker of savory tempeh "bacon", lettuce, tomato, avocado, carrots, sprouts & soy-mayo on multi-grain bread.

The food at *M Cafe de Chaya* is magnificent and I made sure I got enough food so I could take some away for my flight to New York tomorrow. Thurston Moore from *Sonic Youth* was at the cafe as was a guy from *Entourage* so obviously it's the place to be seen at. Holly and I then went home, caught up on computer work and stayed up way too late chatting.

Friday 29 July: Burbank to Phoneix, Arizona to New York

I rose way too early at 04:00 for a 06:10 flight from Burbank airport. Holly dropped me off at Burbank and we said our goodbyes. I ate my takeaway food from *M Cafe de Chaya* on the plane, we stopped at Phoenix, Arizona and I slept on plane. I arrived in New York at 18:00 where Ethan met me at the subway.

My US adventures - Part Six: New York & Troy

Friday 29 July: Arrival in New York & Blossom

I arrived in New York from Los Angeles at 18:00. I caught the air train from JFK airport to the subway where my good friend Ethan met me. Ethan lives in Brooklyn so we trained it there, dropped off my luggage and then caught the train to have dinner at *Blossom* with Ethan's girlfriend, Daphne. Our waiter for the night was friend Joshua's (from *The Discerning Brute*) partner James who is a dancer and a lovely guy. I had the raw Autumn Sweet Potato Rolls US$11 coconut noodles, jicama, carrot, red and yellow pepper, scallion, avocado, almond ginger dipping sauce. Daphne had the Warm Spinach Salad US$14 tempeh bacon, crumbled soy fillet, grilled Asian pear, citrus dressing. Ethan had the Penne Rustica US$17 roasted eggplant, shitake mushrooms, slow roasted tomatoes, olives, jalapeño, fresh basil, shaved tapioca mozzarella.

For dessert Daphne had three scoops of ice cream: coffee, chocolate and peanut for US$9. Ethan and I both had the signature Chocolate Cake $US6. Then we went back to Ethan's and went to sleep. It was an exhausting day of travel.

Saturday 30 July: Brooklyn, Daphne's cooking & Lula's Sweet Apothecary

Just before lunchtime, Ethan, Daphne and I walked over to the Farmers market in Brooklyn where we bought some goodies so that Daphne could make us some lunch. We took the train to Daphne's in Manhattan where she worked in her small, hot kitchen. A *FaceBook* friend of mine, Rachel and I had just been getting to know each other better online recently due to our geeking out on some music and external hard drive issues. We had also spoken on the phone a few times since I arrived in the US and I knew we would get on fabulously when we finally met, and we did. Rachel joined the three of us for lunch.

Daphne is a personal chef and she runs a catering company called *Verite Catering* in New York. Daphne made us some waffles with banana, chocolate syrup and maple syrup. Yum. Ethan is very spoilt due to dating a personal chef and since I was staying with him, I too was spoiled! Rachel and I caught up on a lot of chitchat when Daphne was slaving in her small, hot kitchen.

For dinner Daphne made Corn bread, Roasted eggplant with caramelised onion and basil and Jambalayh consisting of bell peppers, tempeh, corn, zucchini and squash, served with brown dirty rice. Fortunately Daphne has just as much of a sweet tooth as Ethan and I, so we had banana soft serve with chocolate sauce for dessert. I also took some cute photos of Daphne's dog friend, Cookie.

After a few hours we all decided that a trip to *Lula's Sweet Apothecary* was a must. On my US adventures last year to New York with Denis, we ended up going to *Lula's* quite a bit with Ethan as he is obsessed. I had the chocolate ice cream twist with ginger cookies mixed through. Ethan had a cake mix ice cream and cone. Daphne had the fairy floss ice cream and Rachel had similar to mine with chocolate ice cream mixed with marshmallows and pecans. Yum. After *Lula's* Ethan and I caught the train back to Brooklyn, stayed up talking for awhile and then went to sleep.

Sunday 31 July: Terri & more of Daphne's cooking

Ethan and I caught up on a bit of computer work before starting the day with brunch at *Terri* an all organic, vegetarian place. I ordered a Live Long and Green juice US$5.97 that unfortunately was pre-packaged as well as a mixed salad US$6.84 that was also pre-packaged. Ethan ordered the Sunset Proposal smoothie with pineapple, mango, banana, coconut, orange juice, soymilk and the Breakfast Scramble US$7.81 which was great; scrambled tofu, Italian "sausage", spinach, Daiya cheddar, hot sauce.

After brunch we headed to Daphne's for dinner where Daphne cooked for Ethan, Rachel, Daphne's sister Christine, myself and her. We had Chives soup, Spinach curry with peas and sweet potato; Bamboo, straw mushrooms and tempeh; Rice noodles with peanut butter and spices; Deep fried okra with paprika, cayenne and sea salt. Then Creme brule for dessert and some cupcakes.

We were all very full after Daphne's great meal. If you're in New York and need catering, make sure you check out what Daphne has to offer at *Verite Catering*. Ethan and I went home and I caught up on some computer work.

I have just come to the realisation that I have been to the exact same places on my 2011 US adventures as I had on last year's adventures, being Los Angeles, Portland, Seattle, New York (with my Washington trip last year as well.) Even though it's been great to see my friends in all these places for a lot longer time than last year, I feel as though I'm missing out on a lot of things and need to visit more of the country I'm in. I had a great conversation with Peter about going on another road trip together, this time across the middle of the country from New York to my next stop Portland for the *Vida Vegan Bloggers* conference. Sounds like a good plan. I will sleep on it and have a look if it's doable in the morning.

Monday 1 August: Road trip plans & Mexican feast

Today I stayed in at Ethan's to catch up on a lot of computer work and to work out my next moves on my US adventures. Peter and I decided to go on a road trip from Chicago to Portland, so we're in the process of working out the exact details. Can't wait! I had leftover corn bread for lunch.

Daphne came back to Ethan's to cook us a Mexican feast for dinner. Daphne also taught me how to cut properly. Our Mexican feast consisted of tortillas eaten like a burrito with refried beans, brown rice, tomatoes, cremini mushrooms, jalepenos, coriander (cilantro), avocado/guacamole, lettuce, corn with onions and cashew cheese. Yum.

Tuesday 2 August: New York adventures with Rachel, Veg Tuesdays and Soy & Saki

Today was girl's day out with Rachel, my New York tour guide. We met at Union Square and walked via Washington Square Park where I met some SQUIRRELS. We walked to *Sacred Chow* in West Village where we had lunch consisting of Lemon Tahini Hummus US$5 which we asked to be gluten free so they gave us more vegetables. Rachel and I ordered 3 items from the Tapas menu for US$18: Korean Tofu Cutlets with steamed kale - thin slices of tofu baked with Korean maple syrup glaze with garlic, onion, clilies and sesame oil; Dijon Marinated Raw Kale - kale massaged with house Dijon dressing to soften texture and make it taste cooked; and Sautéed Shiitake Mushroom - slowly steamed in garlic oil and soy sauce, served with South Indian dip and sunflower seeds. The food was really good.

Then Rachel and I wandered around SoHo, went to the *Mac* store so that Rachel could get her *iPod* fixed. We waited for ages for her to see someone, so I attended a presentation in the theatre section on music and sound. Then we went to *Aveda* to get the *Aveda* Men's grooming clay for my hair, a product that Jasmin from *Our Hen House* suggested I get.

Then we went to *Snice* in SoHo for a sweet snack. I had a peach smoothie US$5.50 and a chocolate cupcake. *Snice* make the BEST cupcakes I've *ever* tasted! I also ordered a brownie to takeaway. We then headed to a few vintage shops, to *Blue Stockings*, a feminist, activist, book store and then to *MooShoes* where there were a few resident cats. Rachel wanted a gluten free cookie sandwich, so we headed to *BabyCakes* to get one for her. So much walking around today and I now have a thong (flip-flop) tan on my feet - this is something I tease my sister about when she has it as it's *really bogan*, so obviously it's karma that I should also get a tan on my feet.

Daphne organises *Veg Tuesdays* as part of the *NYC Vegan Meetup* group and her company, *Verite Catering*. *Veg Tuesdays* take place most Tuesdays at *Vig Bar* in SoHo, New York with a different theme each week. This week the theme was Business Networking. Yay. I'm sure I can do that! Danny from *V Spot* restaurant had Colombian Empanadas for sale US$4: potato, carrot, onion, coriander (cilantro), corn, Latin seasoned seitan and served with fresh salsa. There were about 40 people who attended, with each person having to stand up and give an elevator pitch for their website, services or product. It was a fun event and I caught up with a few of my New York *FaceBook* friends.

After the event, Rachel and I headed to a late dinner at my favourite restaurant in New York, *Soy and Sake*. Just to prove how obsessed the Americans are with peanuts and peanut butter - there are even peanuts in the nori/sushi rolls! Rachel ordered the Spicy Maki combo US$14 consisting of spicy soy tuna, spicy soy salmon and spicy california roll, the combo came with miso soup. I ordered the coconut shrimp as it was something I'd normally not order. US$6 - deep fried soy shrimp battered with shredded coconut served with sweet chilli sauce. I also ordered the Spicy soy tuna and avocado US$6, Mixed vegetable tempura roll with sweet potato, broccoli and asparagus US$6 and the vege roll with asparagus, lettuce, cucumber and avocado US$5.

Rachel and I had a long but extremely enjoyable day in New York. I caught the subway back to Ethan's and finally got home after heading the wrong way. I met some lovely people when catching the subway.

Wednesday 3 August: Train adventures to Connecticut & My extended family

I left early to catch the subway to Union Square and then a train to Connecticut to visit Ursula and Roman, my Dad's cousins. When it was getting close to me leaving Australia for my US adventures, my Mum had written a letter to Ursula to let her know that I would be in New York in August sometime and would meet up with her and her family if possible. Ursula had connected with us on *FaceBook* and now I was heading to meet them in the flesh. Years ago when my family travelled to the US, we had met Ursula's brother, Roman and his first wife, Marzena, who both my sister and I remembered having long hair past her back, she inspired me to have my long hair years ago.

I wrote some postcards to my friends and family back home in Australia when I was on the train - I hope they can read my writing! Roman and Ursuala and Roman's daughter, Valerie picked me up from the train station in New Haven and drove me to Ursula's place in Berlin where I met Roman and Ursuala's mother, Pela, who is my Dziadek's (grandfather in Polish) sister. I met Roman's wife, Sandy and their son, Steve. Plus Ursula's husband Andy and their boys Michael and Chris.

For lunch, Ursula had bought some *Don Lee Farms* vegan burgers with broccoli and potato bread as well as made some salads including broccoli rabe with garlic, spinach and mushroom plus a sprouted bean trio salad. Ursula also made a lovely black grape, apricot and plum juice. We had some family photos taken of Roman, Sandy, Pela, Valerie, Chris, Ursula and myself.

I spent a few hours with the family, then Roman, Ursula, Valerie and Pela drove me back to New Haven where I trained it back to Union Square and then to Brooklyn where I caught up on computer work and editing of videos. I am having some issues with the lack of space on my *MacBook Pro* at the moment. My videos are taking up too much space and I've been deleting some files, but think I should probably get a small external hard drive for while I'm away.

Thursday 4 August: Cowgirl's Baking, LifeThyme, V Spot & Alas Café

Today I met Andy near his office and Danielle who just flew in from LA for lunch. They run *Sparrow Media* and Danielle also runs the *Galapagus Preservation Society*. We were aiming to catch up with a mutual friend of ours, Daniel for lunch as well but ended up eating without him at *Cowgirl's Baking* where Rachel works. Andy ordered two blackened "fish" tacos - vegan cajun fish, vegan fish sauce, guacamole, pico de gallo, and cabbage and one "chicken" taco - vegan chicken, beans, pico de gallo, daiya cheese, lettuce, and vegan sour cream US$3 each. Danielle ordered two "fish" tacos US$3 each - vegan fish, vegan fish sauce, pico de gallo, & lettuce. I ordered the Avocado and Sprout sandwich US$8 with avocado, sprouts, *Vegenaise*, tomato, lettuce and crispy whole wheat toast. I also ordered a chocolate chip cookie to takeaway and a Talk, Dark and Spicy cupcake chocolate cake with spicy chocolate frosting, chocolate drizzle, and red pepper flakes sprinkled on top, both for US$4.65.

Daniel then met us after lunch, plus Rachel had finished a *PETA* demonstration so she joined us as well. Daniel, Rachel, Danielle and I walked Andy back to his work and then headed to Washington Square Park to interview Danielle and (one of my favourite things) stalk squirrels for photographs. Daniel, Rachel and I headed to *LifeThyme Natural Market* for a juice. I got a lemon, apple, ginger and cayenne juice. I also got some cute photos of Rachel and I and myself and Dan just outside *LifeThyme*.

Rachel and I then trained it to *V Spot* restaurant in Park Slope to interview Danny, this is also my 100th video on my YouTube channel - so *be excited*! After the interview Rachel and I spent way too much time in a pre-loved boutique store, *Beacon's Closest* and only came away with two dresses each! I bought a lovely new (mostly) red dress and another white dress, both halters. Rachel and I were getting quite hungry so decided to stop at *Wholefood* to get some food from their self-serve salad and hot food bar.

Rachel and I then went to *Lula's Sweet Apothecary* to meet Ethan and Ashley and her friend, Katie who are both from *PETA*. While we were waiting, David from *Obsessive Compulsive Cosmetics* walked by so I chatted to him for a bit. We had met at last year's Animal Rights Conference in Washington, DC. *Obsessive Compulsive Cosmetics* is a 100% vegan and cruelty-free professional makeup brand who have many stockists worldwide, I've even used their products in my *How to do professional Mermaid Makeup* video tutorial!

Ethan decided to head back to his place for dinner. Andy and Daniel also popped by *Lula's*, so we all headed to Thompkins Square where I interviewed Ashley who is not only the campaign manager for *PETA*, but friend Will Potter's lovely girlfriend. After the interview, Ashley and Katie said goodbye and Rachel, Andy, Dan and I headed to *Atlas Cafe*, Andy's favourite place in New York. I ordered a chocolate mousse brownie US$3.21. Andy had the vegan Philly steak sandwich with no cheese US$6.95.

After a late dinner, Rachel and I went to *Best Buy* to buy a 750MB external HD. I keep meeting some really great people on the subway on my way home late at night or early in the morning, tonight was no exception.

Friday 5 August: Hanging out with Marissa, Angelica Kitchen, Stogo, Willamsburg, Caravan of Dreams & Lula's

Today I caught up with the lovely Marisa who is about to release her documentary, *Vegucated*. I had seen the documentary and met Marisa at the Animal Rights conference in LA and would also be attending another sneak peak of *Vegucated* before the *Vida Vegan Bloggers* Conference in Portland, OR. Marisa and I met at Union Square at the front of the Andy Warhol statue. We walked around the farmers market and found a place to do our interview before lunch.

Marisa and I then spent way too long at the local post office waiting in line getting a form filled out (and entered into the computer) to post a parcel back home, plus stamps for my postcards I wrote when on the train to New Haven the other day. After this we went to *Angelica Kitchen* a great organic vegan restaurant that has been open since before I was born in 1976. Marisa spotted actress, Maggie Gyllenhall at one of the tables, so it's obviously the place to be seen. We ordered a couple of meals to share. Olé Man Seitan - homemade seitan & roasted vegetable mix folded into a warm whole wheat tortilla, dressed with spicy traditional mole sauce (peanuts & chocolate) and lime-jalapeño tofu sour cream, garnished with pimento. US$14.50. Still Special

- Phyllo Turnover with sauteed leeks, baby bok choy, broccoli rabe, yellow squash, zucchini, carrots, French lentils topped with lemon, basil, parsley pesto and served with balsamic beet marmalade; with green and yellow wax beans and teenage lettuce US$10.

Both these meals were great, thanks Marisa! We were still able to fit in ice cream around a few corners at *Stogo* an all vegan ice cream stop. Marisa had the Oatmeal raisin cookie with Salted caramel pecan ice creams US$4.25. I had the Mexican spiced chocolate and the Pomegranate chocolate chip US$4.25. Both were divine.

After Marisa and I said our goodbyes, I took the train to Willamsburg to meet Joshua Katcher who runs a great blog for the men folk called *the Discerning Brute*, also has an online shop and releases *Pinnacle* magazine focusing on the use of fur in fashion. Joshua is also a very environmentally aware vegan, which I love. I interviewed him as well as a lovely lass, Leanne Mai-Ly Hilgart who designs wonderful eco-conscious clothing and who I'd met at last year's Animal Rights conference in Washington, DC. I was excited to catch up again with her, speak to her about her upcoming *Vaute Couture* collection and more.

After I hung out with Joshua and Leanne, I caught a train back to Union Square where I met Rachel and we headed to dinner at *Caravan of Dreams*. They always have amazing food and service here but I can't stand when the lighting is *so* low, it's bad for getting good photos as I much prefer natural light. Anyway, here's what we ate: The waiter served us radish in olive oil while we were making out minds up, different, unusual, but good. Then we ordered a couple of meals to share. Live Nachos US$12 - chia chips, guacamole, salsa, olives and almond cream. Zucchini and Yellow Squash Spaghetti, Live US$17 - brazil nut & sesame meatballs, sun-dried tomato marinara, kalamata olives and basil.

We then met Ethan at Thompkins Square before he headed to dinner at *Caravan of Dreams* with Daphne and some of her friends. Rachel and I would meet them there for dessert. Not before we went to a great eco store, *Sustainable NYC* that I know a lot of my friends back home would love. When we met Ethan, Daphne and their friends back at *Caravan of Dreams* Rachel had the Chocolate cake with strawberry puree US$9 and I had the Raw Cacao Fudge US$8 - rich dark cacao sweetened with agave nectar. Then we went to Lula's for dessert, as Ethan is obsessed (no matter what he says!)

Saturday 6 August: Hanging out with Ethan, V Spot, Snice & Prospect Park

The past few days since getting my 750MB external HD I've been moving around my videos as well as catching up on editing and writing bits and pieces of my blogs. Daphne and Rachel were busy today and tonight in the Hamptons as Daphne's *Verite Catering* company was catering the *Physicians Committee for Responsible Medicine* fundraising event. I caught up on a bit of computer work with Ethan before we walked to *V Spot* in Park Slope for late brunch about 3pm. I ordered a Ginger Squeeze juice with apple, ginger and lemon US$6. I was trying not to *just* have pancakes for breakfast, so decided to have a little Tofu Ranchero starter US$4 with vegetable tofu scramble, black beans, salsa and avocado on top of a crispy corn tortilla.

My pancake ended up being two pancakes with sausage, so I ate as much as I could and took the rest back for leftovers: Whole wheat pancake with vegan butter and maple syrup and sausage. Ethan ordered the Home Fries US$4 potatoes grilled with rosemary, onion and paprika as well as the Chocolate Chip pancakes US$10.

To walk off our brunch, we walked around Parks Slope, went for a look at the *Brooklyn Superhero Shop* - we even got to see their hidden room at the back! Then went to *Snice*, Parks Slope to get takeaway for dinner, I got a burrito. We then walked around Prospect Park. It was great to see so many families out and about enjoying the beautiful weather and the park. Ethan and I stayed up late working on computer stuff plus I tried to catch up on some video editing.

Sunday 7 August: NYC Vegan Meetup potluck & Candle 79

It sounds boring, but I once again started the day with computer work before Ethan and I caught the train from Brooklyn to Manhattan to go to Daphne's place to attend the *NYC Vegan Meetup* group pot luck. Rachel and I went off to buy some food. I bought salsa, corn chips and stone fruit (which for my US friends means fruit that has stones eg peaches, plums, nectarines etc.) I thought I was a poser with the camera but I'm certain Rachel is much worse. So Rachel took photos of me and made me take a heap of her. Not only are the two of us posers but so is Daphne's dog friend, Cookie, so we took photos of him too.

There were about 30 people who attended the event and great food was on offer. After cleaning up Daphne's place, the four of us headed to dinner at *Candle 79* but not before getting some photos together. Our dinner at *Candle 79* consisted of a complimentary bruscetta-type mini snack for the four of us. Ethan and Daphne shared a side of grilled corn and smoked paprika US$8; the Guacamole Timbale - chipotle black beans, caramelized onions, cucumber-tomato salsa, tortilla chips with ranchero sauce US$8; as well as the Lasagne Special - shredded seitan, cashew and tofu cheese, shallots, mushrooms, truffle tomato basil sauce and sauteed greens. I had the Live Heirloom Tomato-Zucchini Lasagne - cashew cheese, marinated wild mushrooms, heirloom tomato sauce, basil-pine nut pesto US$22. Rachel had the Stuffed Avocado - baby greens, quinoa, zucchini, cucumber, corn, crunchy sprouts, grape tomatoes, radishes, toasted pumpkin seeds with chipotle-avocado dressing US$16.

Ethan ordered the Cannoli for dessert - chocolate cream filling, vanilla chocolate chip ice cream with chocolate drizzle US$12. Rachel and I both ordered the Mexican Chocolate Brownie - caramelized bananas, vanilla mole ice cream, toasted pecans and chocolate-ancho sauce US$12. As tonight was my last night in New York, Ethan and I stayed up way too late talking.

Monday 8 August: Snice, MegaBus to Albany & Honest Weight Food Co-Op

Today I met two of my new favourite friends, Jasmin and Mariann from *Our Hen House* at *Snice*, Soho. Jasmin always says that the two of us were separated at birth and live over other sides of the world. We have a lot in common and it's always great to spend time with her as well as her partner, Mariann. They were both on their juicing cleanse - inspired by the *Fat, Sick and nearly Dead* documentary that day so I ordered a focaccia and ate it in front of them. Then the three of us walked to a spot to film our interview. I then headed to the *MegaBus* depot where I waiting in the heat (no covers, some people were almost fainting) for my bus to Albany to visit Sheila who Peter and I had gone on an amazing road trip with at the beginning of my US adventures. There was WIFI on the bus so I caught up on blog and email work.

Sheila met me at the station and we caught a few buses to the *Honest Weight Food Co-Op* in Albany where we bought the following salads to share for US$15. Because Sheila is a member and volunteers at the co-op we got a 24% discount on all products. Rawsome vegetable salad - beets, carrots, onion, broccoli, red and green bell peppers, vinegar, olive oil, lemon juice, tomatoes, garlic, basil, oregano, salt and black pepper. Sweet potato bakes - sweet potato, curry, coconut, cayenne, olive oil, canola oil, sea salt. Vegetables and Barley - pearled barley, red onions, yellow squash, zucchini, red peppers, green beans, olive oil, balsamic vinegar, sea salt, pepper, parsley. Spicy chickpea salad: chickpeas, tomatoes, red onion, cucumber, jalepenos, canola oil, olive oil, cayenne, cumin and lemon juice. Nick's broccoli salad - broccoli, carrots, onion, red pepper, fakin' bacon (tempeh), *Vegenaise*, apple cider vinegar, lemon juice, garlic, salt, black pepper. Spelt berry and rice - short grain brown rice, spelt berries, soy sauce, sesame oil, carrots, walnuts, currants, red onion, parsley. Santa Fe-style roasted poblano (chili) and corn salad - sweet corn, poblanos, cilantro, tomatoes, red onion, olive oil, lime juice, cumin, oregano, cayenne, salt.

We went back to Sheila's place and caught up on what had been happening in each other's lives since we hung out in LA. I also showed Sheila Justin's karaoke photos from when we were in LA and proceeded to laugh so much at a few of our photos. It's great to hang out with Sheila again.

Tuesday 9 August: Troy with Sheila, X's to O's Bakery & Lil Buddha

I was wrestling with a few external hard drive issues in the morning before we headed to Sarah Preston's vegan bakery, where Sheila also works. *Xs to Os Bakery* in Troy is just walking distance and down the road from where Sheila lives. We had a sandwich with black bean and lentil hummus, tomato, kale, onion and carrots. And, because it's something I'd normally not eat, a Tofu *McYummy* consisting of an English muffin, nutritional yeast cheese, *Yves* Canadian "bacon", grilled and seasoned tofu. Also had a blondie shared with Sheila - which is now my favourite dessert. And, yes, even though it's boring, I ordered a vanilla cupcake with vanilla icing, mostly because of the blue sparkles on top. Yum. And a chocolate brownie.

Upstairs, Sarah has set up a great *Collar City* info shop with a LOT of different 'zines from a lot of different people and organisations. Then Sheila and I went to *Lil Buddha Cafe* for a juice as we'd had too much sugar. We ordered watermelon, grapefruit, ginger and spinach juices 16oz for US$5.50. Sheila and I shared the nachos, which were great - organic flax seed blue corn chips, organic brown rice, beans, melted cheddar *Daiya*, tomatoes, organic greens topped with homemade salsa fresca and avocado US$9.71.

Tonight was all about booking my next road trip adventures with Peter. What had started off as us both meeting in Chicago and driving to Portland, Oregon became me flying to Chicago, Peter flying to Milwaukee with me picking up the rental car from Chicago and driving *by myself* in another country (who drive on the wrong side of the road) to pick Peter up in Milwaukee and then we'd drive to Portland. Phew. I had also decided to leave New York on Thursday night. So Thursday and Friday are going to be exhausting...

Wednesday 10 August: Troy potluck

I stayed in today to catch up on computer work, editing and such. When Sheila got home from work, we listened to Fleetwood Mac (!) and made some dinner for the potluck her and her housemate, Rachel were hosting. I took some great photos of Rachel's cat friends, Bella (also known as Pudding) and Cleo (also known as Moon Bear).

Dinner was Mac and Cheese with different types of pasta, different cheese including *Daiya*, pepper, *Earth Balance* butter, nutritional yeast and hazelnut milk. I made a raw salad with beetroot leaves, grated beetroot and carrot, spinach and kale from the garden, avocado and lemon. Rachel made a curry with coconut, basic curried rice with creamed peppers and zucchini from the garden. For dessert Rachel made Strawberry Shortcake. A few of Rachel and Sheila's friends dropped by for a bit, ate some food and chatted. It wasn't too late a night.

Thursday 11 August: X's to O's Bakery, EMPAC, Loving Café, MegaBus to NYC, Terri & Journey to Chicago

Today was Sheila and my day to hang out with our mutual friend, Jared who I had interviewed in LA. First stop was obviously *Xs to Os Bakery* where Sarah had made an amazing chocolate cake I just had to take a photo of. Jared had an Elvis cupcake with peanut butter. I had another McYummy and a banana cream cupcake.

Then we walked to the *Experimental Media and Performing Arts Centre (EMPAC)* where Sheila used to study and work. Her friend, Ryan met us there and gave us a great tour of the concert hall, theatre and studios. A lot of my music friends would *love* this place.

We then headed to a *Loving Hut* restaurant in Delmar: *Loving Cafe*. Sheila ordered a Peach and Green Tea with almond milk smoothie US$4.49, spring rolls US$2.99 for 4 and the Chick n Wrap with garlic pesto, served with chips (crisps) and coleslaw US$6.95. Jared ordered a Lemonade swirl smoothie and the Chick n Sub with pepper jack cheese, served with chips (crisps) and coleslaw US$6.99. I ordered a banana smoothie with almond milk US$4.49 and the chicken with sesame seed oil, organic noodles and a side of vegetables for US$6.99.

The meals were great but the overuse of plastic and throwaway containers was annoying. Vegan food is better for the environment, except when there's excessive packaging, and depending where the food is sourced. Jared then drove us to the *MegaBus* station where I was catching the bus at 18:30 to head back to New York. We had a bit of time until my bus arrived so we sat under a tree near the *Amtrak* station. I did some quick tarot readings for Sheila and Jared, then we said our goodbyes and I left. I had a great time with Sheila and will miss her a great deal.

I caught up on editing of videos on the *MegaBus* as the WIFI wasn't working for some reason. Ethan and Daphne met me when I arrived in New York at 21:15 and we walked to *Terri* for dinner. Daphne ordered the Roasted Vegetable sandwich as a salad - eggplant, squash, sun dried tomato, peppers, kalamata olives and balsamic vinegar US$7.81. Ethan ordered a *Terri* Berri smoothie with strawberries, raspberries, blueberries, soymilk and agave US$6.43 and the Bacon Ceddar Chicken Ranch sandwich with "chicken", soy bacon, *Daiya* cheddar, ranch sauce and lettuce US$7.81. I ordered the Breakfast Scramble (that Ethan ate last week and I enjoyed) US$7.81 scrambled tofu, Italian "sausage", spinach, *Daiya* cheddar, hot sauce.

I said goodbye to Ethan and Daphne, headed to the gym next door to have a shower and then got on the train to head to LaGuardia airport. When I was sitting at the train station I was chatting to a lovely lady, Dolly who is an acupuncturist. Dolly ended up getting off at my station, hailing a cab and heckling the driver for a good price to the airport plus it turned out that she's friends with my friend Marisa - what a small world. When I got to the airport it was after midnight and no one was checking in luggage. Thus began my waiting for my flight at the LaGuardia airport for my flight to Chicago...

My US adventures - Part Seven: Road trip from Chicago to Portland

Friday 12 August: New York to Chicago, Chicago to Milwaukee, Indian Lake park, Don Quinn, Spook Cave

Due to no one checking in luggage because no one was working until 04:00, I was in for a lot of waiting around for my flight at LaGuardia airport in New York. However luckily I spoke to Holly for over an hour on the phone, my sister for a bit and a lady at the airport for awhile. She was a bit fragile but fine to talk to someone different for awhile, until she started pushing the word of the Lord etc onto me. The phone saved me, thanks Louie! By the time 04:00 came around I hadn't slept or done any work I had hoped I would catch up on. Then I caught a shuttle bus with another lady (who has a vegan daughter in Europe) to the actual area where we would board our flight to Chicago. The 06:00 flight couldn't come soon enough and I slept the whole flight to Chicago.

I arrived at O'Hare airport about 07:00, got my bag and waited for the shuttle bus to take me to my rental car place, that was closer to Midway airport than to where I'd flown into. I had already booked my ticket to Chicago by the time Peter and I realised that it was better timing for him to fly from Seattle to Milwaukee (instead of to Chicago) and the car rental from Milwaukee was more expensive than from Chicago. So, I had to use all of my adventurous spirit and drive *by myself* in another country on the *wrong side* of the road from Chicago, Illinois to pick up Peter in Milwaukee in the next state North, Wisconsin. I drive interstate all the time when back in Brisbane, so I was sure I'd be fine. I made up a *Jimmy Eat World* MP3 mix CD, I knew the car was an automatic and I would just take my time as I wasn't in a rush.

So I picked up the *Aveo, Chevrolet* on South Archer Avenue and left around 10:30. I merged onto the I55 then the I90 and I94 to Wisconsin. I had a few beeps from a few cars, normally something I would ignore, but as I had the windows down with the wind caressing my hair, I was able to ask one of the truck drivers why he was beeping me. He said it was because I was going to the right a bit over the line. Noted. Did my best to fix this. Finally picked up Peter (*I made it!*) at around 12:30 at the General Mitchell airport and he took over the driving.

We drove to Madison where there's a *WholeFoods*, Peter knows where every *WholeFoods* is supposedly. We ate our lunch in a park nearby before we drove to the *beautiful* Indian Lake park. The view was beautiful, I took some photos and Peter freaked out about a bee. Due to both of us not sleeping for much over the past day or so, we ended up finding a spot at the park and slept for a few hours on the blanket we'd bought at a thrift store earlier.

Around sunset we started our travels again, this time we found a place around Dodgeville that had a huge plane, known as the *Don Quinn* that was stationed outside an inn. I took a photo of Peter on the wing and some others inside. Inside the plane was quite amazing. It's a Boeing C-97 built in 1952 that was used during the Korean war for transporting people. 150 people could fit in this plane. Due to the economical - not to mention environmental - issues of burning 600 gallons of fuel per hour, the plane was no longer needed by the US government and *Don Quinn* (the Inn) purchased it in 1977.

Peter wanted hash browns and as we didn't find them at the inn near the plane, we found a casino on board a boat that was quite a miserable place. I abhor gambling in all forms, plus add in some inside smoking to the equation and it wasn't that great a place, but something I can at least say I've now experienced. When we were driving on Highway Number 18, making up silly songs about heartbreak and the road, we saw a baseball game at a park somewhere in Cobb so decided we'd check it out. I'm not really into sport much at all (except for Australian Football League - AFL) but we had a great time watching the locals throwing and hitting at balls and trying to work out the rules.

We played on the swings and other fun things at the park where the baseball game took place, continued our trek on Highway Number 18, with more heartbreak songs created and found a place near *Spook Cave*, McGregor to stay the night. It was a beautiful night with all the signs of tomorrow night's full moon and even though it started raining early in the morning and the land owner almost drove over us with his tractor, we had a good night to an end of a long couple of days. I really want to be woken up by a deer licking my face. This didn't happen.

Saturday 13 August: Pottsville, Charles City, Des Moines, Best Place Ever, Bold Native screening & A Dong

In the morning after the tractor incident, we parked for awhile at the Spook Cave campgrounds for Peter to catch up on some more sleep and for me to explore a bit, have a shower and breakfast. Then we headed to Pottsville, Iowa where Peter had read a book, *Postville: A Clash of Cultures in Heartland America* by Stephen G Bloom, on the Jewish community who ran a slaughterhouse in the area, which was meant to be now abandoned. It didn't seem to be abandoned to me at all. We later found out that the slaughterhouse had been reopened by another Jewish company. Luckily it was the Sabbath and no one was there. One of us was scared of the rats in the ceiling... and it wasn't me. Just saying. We then drove to Charles City where we stopped at a lovely coffee shop to catch up on computer work. The guy there played some wonderful music such as Edith Piaf, Judy Garland, Frank Sinatra and other of my favourite standards singers. It was a great place to stop.

One of Peter's friends in Des Moines, Iowa, Adam owns a great lil' film store, *Best Place Ever* on 24th Street. Due to us coming through town, Adam decided to organise a screening of Denis' film, *Bold Native* (Peter has a small part in) so that Peter could answer some questions after the film. First, though, Peter was a guest on Brisbane-based Carolyn Bailey's *ARZone* a website that has weekly live guest chat interviews with vegan activists. I have wanted to take part in the Q&As at *ARZone* but due to them being Sunday morning (Australian time) I normally have plans, don't want to be near my computer or am sleeping in. So it was great to see how the live chat works and how many people get involved. The whole event was very long though, over two hours in the end. You can read Peter's transcript on the ARZone website.

It was great to watch *Bold Native* again, see many of my friends with big and small parts and just enjoy a really good film. Adam's *Best Place Ever* store holds regular screenings and events, so drop by if you're in Des Moines. *Bold Native* is also now on *NetFlix*, so check it out if you haven't. I interviewed Denis about *Bold Native* on my road trip with him to New York last year.

After the screening, Peter and I headed to a local Vietnamese restaurant, *A Dong*, with Dan who ended up being a *FaceBook* friend of mine (small world, love it!) and Dan's friend, Ryan.

Ryan orderd the Cha Gio Chay - spring rolls US$2.50 along with the Com Chien Duong Chan Chay - fried rice US$6.75. Peter ordered the Com Tau Hu Xao Hanh - stir fried Mongolian tofu with crispy noodles and steamed rice US$6.75. I ordered the Com Tau Hu Xao Cai Ngot - stir-fried tofu and yo-choy (like gai lan) with steamed rice US$6.75 which was just what I needed. Dan ordered the Com tan Hu Don Chay - stuffed tofu with tomato sauce topping and rice US$7.

Peter and I were staying at his friend, Justin's place that night, but didn't feel like sleeping just yet, so we parked the car at Justin's and walked around the town of Des Moines a bit, through the park and college where we found a rabbit just hanging out on the grass. She/he let me get up pretty close for a photo. Really cute. Peter and I walked back to Justin's and slept well.

Sunday 14 August: Iowa State Fair & the Butter Cow, PayPal & York

In the morning I had a shower, made some banana toast and painted my nails until Peter woke up. Adam and his partner, Amanda came over to tell us about the Iowa State Fair and the Butter Cow - a cow carved out of *butter* - that had caused a bit of controversy with local animal activists sticking a *Go Vegan* sign earlier that morning onto the cow.

The media really embraced this story, with the *Des Moines Register* article being the one most people quoted from, plus a poem *An Ode to the State Fair Butter Cow Battle*, and the story even made it to the *NPR* morning edition. Peter and I copied the fair entry stamps (from Adam and Amanda) on our wrists as I had to experience at least one fair when in the US and there was no way I was paying for it. The four of us headed to a local coffee shop where Justin met us and then Peter and I said our goodbyes and went to the fair.

Now, this fair is meant to be the biggest in the US, but it didn't seem that big. Maybe it was due to it being after 5pm on Sunday when we finally got there, but it was even smaller than Brisbane's Ekka. I took a photo of the view when we were on the monorail. It was fun. Peter doesn't like heights.

When we were walking out of the fair, Peter spotted a jumping castle that seemed to be vacant. I had to get footage of him going to the middle and back then I was meant to do the same. Fortunately there was nothing exciting in the middle, I couldn't actually jump over the first bit, and some kids came along so there's no footage of me, only Peter. Hehe.

Late that night when we were somewhere in Nebraska, Peter gets *very* excited about somewhere he wants to show me that is a huge surprise and I will be very excited about. A big company. "Google headquarters?" I ask. "Umm, no. Wrong state." Whatever. Don't think much else related to companies will excite me, but anyway, what? "It's a surprise." So, after driving around for ages we get to the *PayPal* headquarters in Omaha, Nebraska which is *not* exciting in the slightest bit to me, but Peter is ever so excited which makes it somewhat exciting. Peter forces me to take *many* photos of him on top of the PayPal sign. Now *that* is amusing. We drive for a bit more until we get to York, Nebraska where we stay the night at a truck stop.

Monday 15 August: North Platt thrift store, 9/11 Truth, Boulder, Sun Deli Pizza & Pearl Street Mall

We stopped at a coffee shop in the morning for Peter to get his caffeine fix and for us both to use our laptops then headed to a Goodwill store in North Platt, Nebraska where I bought 3 great dresses for about US$12 total. I was also very excited as the lass at the checkout counter checked my US$20 bill for counterfeit with some sort of magic pen that was similar to a pen I had when I was younger that you drew over the other coloured pens and the colour would change and/or disappear. Fortunately or unfortunately (hmm, not sure which one...) the pen used on my US$20 dollar note did not do a thing, so I was able to leave the store knowing my notes were not counterfeit as well as that the North Platt area was in safe hands. Peter said that these pens don't actually prove anything, and something else about the acidity and paper.

Back on the road we go when we come across a truck with 9/11 Truth written on the side of it. "Get a photo, get a photo!" yells Peter excitedly to which I'm sure I gave a look of uncertainty as to why I would want a photo of a truck whether or not it had 9/11 Truth on the side. By the time I worked out Peter was serious, he had sped up alongside the truck and I went to take the photo, the truck braked fiercely and was not within shutter sight. Fortunately however, soon the truck overtook us and I managed to get a photo. Excited yet?

We were then on our way to Boulder, Colorado where a fan/friend of both mine and Peter's, Ashley had offered for us to stay at her place. Ashley always shares my *FaceBook* and *Twitter* updates and both Peter and I were looking forward to meeting her. Peter was having a snooze in the car when I was driving to Boulder. Ashley gives amazing directions and we were at her place in no time. Peter and I were hungry so Ashley took us to *Sun Deli Pizza and Liquor* for dinner where Peter had the basic cheese steak: grilled baked tempeh steak with *Daiya* cheese served on a wheat roll US$7.49. Ashley and I shared a small Pesto Chicken pizza: pesto sauce, red bell pepper, garlic, Gardein chicken and almond ricotta US$17.99.

I had to get my camera to take a photo of the bathroom as it's pretty impressive with mosaic glass and mirrors on all four walls and fairy lights! I bought some *Hemp I Scream* and spoke to the hippy couple who made the ice cream. They were on their way to *HempFest* in Seattle to meet their son and they had a great travel vehicle. After dinner we walked into Pearl Street mall, the main area of Boulder where we wandered around, watched some roaming performers, including a guy who juggled knives and did acrobatic tricks on stretched wire. Me oh my. He had quite a crowd. Ashley and I ate the ice cream. Peter said I would love Boulder and I do.

Tuesday 16 August: Central Park, Prairie Dogs, Flaggstaff Mountain, Denver & Watercourse

Not only is Ashley great at giving directions and a great tour guide, but she also cooked us breakfast! We may not want to leave. Ashley made us great scrambled tofu.

The three of us walked around Central Park and headed to the local library where one of the areas looks out over the stream running through the town. Lovely. There was an amazing photographic exhibition of William Corey who I found out later is a Japanese gardens photographer who passed over in 2008. Took a few photos of his photographs. One of Kogen Ji and one of Byodo-In (The Phoenix Temple.) I will one day go to the gardens where both of these photos were taken.

I wanted to meet some prairie dogs and Peter wanted to hang out in a coffee shop with books, so I drove Ashley and I to Arapahoe Road where we saw some real cuties who I took a lot of photos of. Prairie dogs are mighty fast and we were a bit scary I guess, so it was all about taking quick photos and hoping for the best. I took quite a few! After hanging out with the prairie dogs and even a few rabbits, Ashley and I drove up Flagstaff Mountain where we looked over Boulder. The scenery is beautiful. I took various photos along the mountain, at the top of Flagstaff and of the view from on top, looking down over Boulder. Some ladies took a couple of photos of Ashley and I as well.

It was really a lovely drive up the mountain and looking at the scenery. I love to go on road trip adventures back home, just drive and see where the road leads sometimes. My sister and I went on a great trip the Sunday before I left for my US adventures to *Sirromet* winery where we wandered around until it got cold and met *so* many wallabies hanging out near the grape vines. On the drive down the mountain, Ashley spotted a mother deer and her baby on the side of the road. So cute. I got a photo.

Later that afternoon, we picked Peter up and drove to Denver to have dinner with another fan/friend of Peter's and mine, Michael who I'd met at last year's Animal Rights Conference in Washington, DC and who was the first friend I made at last year's ARC. Michael was absolutely devastated when I first shaved my head in March (it was quite a harsh look and a shock for a lot of people) but after my *Twitter* talk at ARC he seems to have warmed to it a bit. It amuses me how attached to my hair a lot of people are. Shaving my head was one of the most liberating things I've ever done and you know, *hair grows back*! I believe the growing back stage is all part of my life lessons in patience.

We met Michael at *Watercourse* restaurant along with Peter's friend, Courtney and her daughter, Erica. We waited about half an hour to get a seat, as *Watercourse* was full and very busy. At least by the time we sat down we knew exactly what we would order. Peter ordered the Burrito US$10.25: whole wheat tortilla stuffed with brown rice, grilled vegetables, asadero (vegan queso cheese) and chorizo (vegan sausage) smothered in green chilli, topped with shredded lettuce and pico de gallo. Michael ordered the sweet chilli "egg" rolls US$8.25: cabbage, tofu, portobello mushrooms, carrot and green onion stuffed in a crispy vegan wrapper, served with sweet chilli mango sauce. Ashley ordered the blackened tofu US$11.95: spiced tofu with coconut cream sauce served with brown rice, broccoli and avocado. I ordered the macro place US$11.95: crispy tofu with teriyaki ginger sauce over brown rice served with steamed greens, arame (kelp) salad and home made pickled cabbage. Ashley and I shared a Chocolate cream pie US$5.

So about this time, my camera decides to stop mostly due to the fact that I'd shown Ashley a lot of my animal photos on our drive to Denver, plus played her the video of Peter going on the jumping castle. So I had to settle for a photo of Michael, myself and Peter from Michael's phone camera.

Wednesday 17 August: Cheyenne, Jackalopes & Devil's Tower

In the morning when I woke, Ashley let me know that I'd missed out on seeing a deer in their backyard - how exciting! I saw her photos. And, Ashley had told me previously that someone she knew had seen a baby bear in a tree somewhere around us. I still haven't seen a bear yet. I caught up on some computer work, before we left the lovely Ashley to settle into her new house with her new flatmates before she started study at *Naropa*. Most of my friends asked me if I would live in America and where I'd like to live. Up until now, I'd never been to somewhere I could see myself living (maybe LA, just because most of my friends in the US are there) until I fell in love with Boulder.

Then Peter and I left my new home, Boulder, Colorado and headed North to Wyoming. We stopped at the new *Wholefoods* on Pearl where we got some takeaway for lunch/dinner. Then we drove around for awhile and I took photos of the scenery.

One of our petrol/gas stops was at Cheyenne where I was finally able to buy a redneck sticker for my friend (since year 6), Benjamin. It was a shooting licence type sticker. I was told to get the more redneck the better. Also, at this rest stop along with a *huge* selection of redneck stickers perpetuating *every* type of stereotype you can think of, there were the *My Family* stickers that are quite popular in Australia. Peter had previously told me about some sort of wild creature native to Wyoming, the Jackalope, which is supposedly some type of rabbit with antlers! Initially I'm, like, *how can a rabbit get antlers?* plus Peter had that look in his eyes when I know that what's being said is not entirely truthful. But, anyway, at this rest stop, I see a postcard with a Jackalope picture on it! So I apologise to Peter for not believing him in the first place.

Peter wanted hash browns and coffee, so we stopped later at the *Outpost Cafe* in Lusk where we ordered hash browns for only US$2.50. In Australia, our hash browns look more like deep fried patties, so I was a bit confused when we got grated potato. I got in trouble for putting tomato sauce on my hash brown, but it was a *love heart*!

We saw an Antelope on our trip around dusk and some deer on the side of the road, this was a common scene at dusk. I took many photos of the sunsets Peter and I shared each day of our adventures. Just lovely. *Devil's Tower* is where we were headed next where *Close Encounters of the Third Kind* was filmed. I took an excessive amount of photos of *Devil's Tower*.

I'd only seen photos of *Devil's Tower* online, in person was much more spectacular. When we drove into the area, there was a tipi near the car park. Both of us said in unison "That's where we should sleep tonight!" The tower is very majestic. It was a beautiful view and the energies were amazing.

Peter and I sat on one of the rocks near the base of *Devil's Tower* and had a picnic for dinner with the food we'd bought from *Wholefoods* when we were in Boulder. It was a lovely, peaceful night, clear sky, wonderful energies until some bats flew over us when we were lying down on said rock. Now, instead of just letting the bats fly by, safe in their travels, Peter absolutely *freaks* out, sits up towards where the bats were flying past, freaks out *even more*, then grabs his stuff and runs away. Peter's account is somewhat different, in that Peter states the bats flew at him/attacked him, of which there is no proof to this version of events. I'll let you make up your own mind on that.

We lay out underneath the stars on our blanket until the temperature dropped and we moved into the tipi. We may or may not have played truth or dare. It was a great night at *Devil's Tower*.

Thursday 18 August: Exploring Devil's Tower, Prairie Dogs Town, Bozeman & Helena

In the morning, we moved into the car when the masses of tourists, hikers and climbers started to arrive with the sunrise. I slept for a bit more, before getting up to explore the area. I went to the information area where I read about *Devil's Tower* and found out that the Native American Indian tribes prefer the name *Bear Lodge* to be used. Also that they don't want people to climb the tower, as it's like climbing *Uluru* (*Ayers Rock*) in Australia's Northern Territory. The Indigenous Australians compare climbing *Uluru* to desecrating a church if you're religious. I'd say this would be the same for climbing *Bear Lodge*. Most white people have no respect for Indigenous cultures. There's a quote at Uluru: *the white man goes there to take pictures rather than going there to listen.* Which brings me to all the great photos I took.

I went into the tipi we'd slept in and did a Tarot reading (King of Pentacles, Swords VIII and Cups Ace) and had some breakfast. When Peter woke up, we walked around the base of *Bear Lodge* with a lot of others on the 1.3 mile (2km) *Red Beds* trail. The scenery and the rock from all the different angles was beautiful.

Then we went to the Prairie Dogs Town close by so that I could get some more photos of prairie dogs, this time I took a heap of photos with prairie dogs standing up, looking at me, coming towards me, in pairs. You can just imagine all the photos I took.

We stopped at a co-op in Bozeman, Montana for dinner before making our way to Helena where Peter's friend, Laura was staying with her then-partner, Matt at Matt's family's property. It was quite late when we arrived in Helena. Laura and Matt met us in town and we followed them to the property on the outskirts of Helena. We chatted for awhile, Matt's sister, Annika and her friends arrived home from partying to entertain us. Peter and Laura stayed up for awhile catching up and I went to bed.

Friday 19 August: Helena, Montana; Hike & Eurotrash party

Today was Annika's 25th birthday and as she was having a party with a Eurotrash theme, Peter and I decided to stay an extra night. I caught up on some computer work before heading to town with Peter, Annika and Laura. Peter and I hung out at a few thrift stores whilst Laura and Annika had pedicures. We then ordered takeaway burritos at *Taco del Sol* (meaning *of the Sun*) 12 inch for US$4.50 with black beans, rice, salsa fresca, lettuce and no cheese so they gave me extra guacamole.

I also really wanted a horchata drink but they didn't have a non-dairy version. We went back to the house, and while the family were preparing for the party, Laura, Peter and I went on a walk around the property. Laura and Matt's family had told me that there had been some bears around the area, so if I was to finally meet a wild bear, it would happen here!

The walk was pretty intense. Peter stopped part of the way along our journey and Laura and

I continued up the hill a bit. There's been a beetle infestation affecting the pine trees on the Robbins' property and other properties that surround. Matt's Dad, Jim Robbins is a published author who also writes for the *New York Times* environmental section, he just wrote an article on the pines turning red from the beetles.

Deciding not to go right up to the top of the hill, Laura and I collected Peter on our way back and made our way back to the house. Peter and I worked on our outfits for the party. I borrowed some clothes from Annika for my Eurotrash look, Peter didn't have to borrow anything. Just saying. It was a fun night, I spoke to a lot of Annika's friends as well as got to know her lovely family some more. At night the weather dropped quite a bit, it was the coldest I'd been for my whole trip, not good.

Saturday 20 August: Rock Creek Lodge, Missoula, Hot Srings at Weir Creek, Three Rivers & Walla Walla

After a sleep in, computer work and getting the directions for a hot spring from Matt and Jim; Peter and I said our goodbyes to the lovely Robbins family and headed towards Idaho. Montana, and especially Helena are very picturesque.

We stopped off at a thrift store in Helena that reminded me of the *Smart Tip* back home. We were driving along for a bit, about to run out of petrol/gas when we came across the *Rock Creek Lodge* - their claim to fame is their annual *Testicle Festival*, where (I quote:) *the festival feeds over 2 ½ tons of bull balls to its many hungry revellers. Not only can you get a taste of these yummy delicious deep-fried bull's testicles, but while you're there, you'll no doubt want to participate in the bull-chip throwing contest, the wet t-shirt or hairy chest competitions, and bull-shit bingo.* Hmm... Obviously we were *devastated* that we wouldn't be around when this festival was taking place!

The petrol bowser had a really dodgy sign saying that the amount the bowser shows was not the correct amount you paid for petrol, rather it was more expensive, and to come into the bar to ask for petrol. So we headed over to the lodge where there were *so many* redneck and offensive stickers on display all over the front of the building, plus a sign stating *No Wimps Allowed*. At a lot of these in the middle of nowhere places Peter and I walk into, everyone will normally look at us when we come in, you know, new people they don't know. Everyone is usually really friendly and accommodating. These people were not. The whole bar turned around, stopped talking and almost glared at us. I asked about the petrol to which the bar tender replied to go down the road to get fuel/gas as it was cheaper - I've never heard of such a thing! Fortunately a couple of dog friends came over to say hi and it took the edge off a bit, but we couldn't wait to get out of there. Also, let it be known, that this would be one of the best ways to gather bodies if you were a serial killer: people almost out of petrol, tell them to go down the road to the next gas station, there isn't one close at all so you have someone waiting there to pick up the people when they run out of fuel, they're in the middle of nowhere not knowing where they are but you do etc. Fortunately for us, there was a gas station quite close with much cheaper petrol - US$1 less - and we're still alive to tell the tale. This was the most uncomfortable situation I'd been in all of my US adventures.

Peter and I drove along to Missoula and had lunch at the *Good Food Store* then we drove towards the hot springs at *Weir Creek*. *Weir Creek* is along *Post Office Creek* near mile marker 142 at Clearwater National Park, Idaho. The trek to the hot spring was about a 30 minute hike up some steep hills. I asked some people camping for some specific directions, as everything looked the same. We were to look out for the white plastic pipe. A family walking back from the spring advised us not to put your whole body in. So of course, when we found the hot spring, I did immerse myself fully and *completely* overheated myself and had to lie on the board to cool down! I had never been to a natural hot spring before, it was really beautiful, calming, therapeutic and really hot with the temperature around 103-110 degrees Fahrenheit (39-43 degrees Celsius.) *Weir Creek* (granite pool) hot spring sits about 50 feet above Weir Creek. No bears though.

We hiked back to the car, then started the drive towards Oregon. We stopped for a look at the *Three Rivers Resort* where there was a lovely deer who came to say hi. We drove around for awhile before finding a place to stay along the highway after Walla Walla near the wineries and before Pasco, Washington.

Sunday 21 August: Last stop on our road trip, Hillsboro

So, I am excited to report that I have been to 14 out of 50 USA states! There's a heap more I'd like to explore, obviously, but I think that's a really great start with just two US adventures (as an adult) under my belt.

Peter and I stopped off at a *Taco del Mar* for brunch that was somewhere in Oregon, maybe The Dalles. I had a taco. The weather was really hot here which was great. We were on our way to our friend, Brittyn's place in Hillsboro, Oregon where I would be staying for most of the rest of my stay in the US. At about this stage I started to realise that I was running out of time on my latest US adventures, a fact I was not too pleased with.

There were a lot of wind turbines on our mid west adventures and I took photos of them. Peter and I stopped at the *WholeFoods* in Portland to get some snacks before driving to Hillsboro where Brittyn had made us some food and where Peter and my mid west adventures came to an end. Peter and I drove from Chicago to Portland in nine days, a total of 2121 miles (3413km). There aren't many people I can handle for more than a couple of days, let alone travel with. Peter and I get on extremely well. We have the important stuff in common and then the rest we balance each other out really well. We always have fun together and I missed him as soon as he left Brittyn's. I had such an amazing time on our road trip! My next adventures however await: hanging out with Brittyn in Portland, Oregon and the Vida Vegan Bloggers Conference - can't wait!

NOTE: A friend in Portland, Mark informed me that the Jackalope (see above Wednesday) is in fact not a real creature at all. After arriving home I did some more research on the topic and Peter Young: I TAKE MY APOLOGY BACK! I should have trusted my initial instinctual response and NOT believed you!

My US adventures - Part Eight: Portland, OR & my last week

Sunday 21 August: Arrival in Portland

In the afternoon, Peter dropped me off at Brittyn's place in Hillsboro, Oregon to end our mid west road trip. He headed back to Chicago, via Seattle, to return the rental car for me (one way rental was an extra US$1000!) which I really appreciated. Brittyn and I walked to the park and the library to get my bearings. I then had a shower and dinner consisting of pasta salad Brittyn said she'd made (I found out later her mother, Sydney had in fact made the meal) and some roasted vegetables I'd bought at *WholeFoods* previously that day. Then I caught up on a bit of computer work and it was bedtime.

Monday 22 August: Sweet Lemon Bistro

Brittyn's cat, Corwin hates me. He hissed at Peter and I yesterday, and kept me from slumber in the early hours of the morning. There is something wrong with him. It took quite awhile to get him ready for the vet, big dramas. Brittyn's Mum, Sydney, picked me up to head to her place to use her WIFI and do my washing. Unfortunately we couldn't locate the WIFI password, so I caught up on editing videos. I had pasta salad that Syd had made previously and an apple for lunch.

Brittyn and I headed to dinner at *Sweet Lemon Vegan Bistro* in Bethany, one of the *Loving Hut* restaurants. We ordered the Heavenly Kabob - charbroiled marinated soy protein with finely grated lemongrass on skewers, sprinkled with sesame seeds US$5. Brittyn ordered the Zen Noodles - marinated tofu, noodles and assorted vegetables served with sweet lemon's sauce

US$8. I ordered Treasure Island - grilled marinated soy protein, tofu and assorted vegetables served on a nest of crispy noodles US$8.

This is a great, friendly place. The food is pretty simple with all of the dishes seeming to be made up of soy protein or tofu, the same sort of assorted vegetables for each meal and served with noodles or rice. This is a much healthier *Loving Hut*-style restaurant than the one in Brisbane. Brittyn and I shared a slice of their lemon cake for dessert and had some of the strawberry cake to takeaway.

Tuesday 23 August: Bullwinkle's with Brittyn & Blossoming Lotus

I did a bit of computer work in the morning before Brittyn and I went to *Bullwinkle's* in Wilsonville around lunchtime to play mini golf (putt putt) for my first time. I am fast becoming to realise that Brittyn is *way* too competitive for me. As in, this is my *first time* playing mini golf, and I never really have cared for winning at all (don't be on a team with me if you do!) as it's all about the experience of the game for me - typical Sagittarius behaviour. Brittyn isn't very good at encouraging her competitor but it was still fun with Brittyn winning with 63 and myself getting 78. Brittyn also got a hole in one, which was pretty exciting!

Then we went go-karting where I was pretty content just going around the track, looking at the excitement on the kids' faces and looking at the scenery, Brittyn became a race-car driver intent on taking out whoever was in her path. Then it was time for the arcade games where Brittyn won air hockey and I won the percussion game that had great Japanese-style songs and versions of popular tunes that you could play on the drum kit to, similar to *Guitar Hero* that I love. We tried the photo booth but the photos were really bad quality unfortunately.

For dinner, we were meeting friends of mine, Mark and Imber (who I had stayed with last year when I staying in Portland) at *Blossoming Lotus*. We were a bit early though, so we dropped by *Scapegoat Tattoo* where my friend, Brian works. It was great to see him and to hear about his tattooing adventures overseas. Brittyn and I then went to a thrift store where I bought a couple of really cute dresses then headed to *Blossoming Lotus*.

Mark ordered the crispy artichoke fritters US$8. I ordered the Live nachos US$10. Imber ordered the Grilled polenta with wild rice US$14 with roasted zucchini, cauliflower, with fennel, sage, tempeh with basil, rosemary and roasted butternut sauce and mixed baby kale. Brittyn & Mark ordered the Fafitas. Brittyn with portobello and veg, Mark with soy curls. I also ordered the Live sorrel pesto and portobello pizza US$13. For dessert Mark had the banana, almond cream cheese layer cake. Brittyn had a coconut passionfruit cupcake. I had the pomegranate raw cheesecake - it was lovely; and Imber had the vanilla soft serve. It was great to have dinner at *Blossoming Lotus* again and it was great to hang out with Mark and Imber.

Wednesday 24 August: Syd's for Dinner & Aggravation

Today I caught up on a lot of blog and computer work when Brittyn was at work. For dinner we went to Syd's place where Brittyn's Mum cooked us a great meal: Lasagne with zucchini, spinach, tomato sauce, onion, tofu, *Daiya* cheese, *Boca* crumbles. Served with garlic bread and a salad of heirloom tomatoes and lettuce with *Trader Joe's* Balsamic Vinaigrette Goddess Dressing.

After dinner Brittyn insisted on playing a game called *Aggravation* that I had never heard of before. Even her own Mother was apprehensive about playing this game knowing full well the extent of her competitiveness. This was a horrible game where you try to get your markers around the game but you may just have to go right back to the start if someone (Brittyn) lands on your marker. Brittyn obviously won. I'm sure Syd knew that nothing helps get over the sting of Brittyn's competitiveness than something sweet to eat, so she served up some *So Delicious* vanilla ice cream with fresh strawberries and roasted hazelnuts. A great way to end the night - thanks for dinner, Syd.

Thursday 25 August: Portland with Robert, Powell's, Prasad, Vendetta Meet and Greet &

Vegucated

I spent the morning working on the computer and catching up on blogging. Robert Cheeke from *Vegan Bodybuilding* picked me up around lunchtime and we headed out and about in Portland. First stop was the amazing *Powell's* bookstore where we first headed to the Fitness section to check that Robert's book was still in stock. Yes it was, so I took quite a few photos of Robert posing with his book. Plus I also rearranged the books, still keeping them in alphabetical order mind you, so that his *Vegan Bodybuilding & Fitness book* was featured – face out. I also wrote a lil' recommendation note for customers with a 5-star rating. I wonder how long it was there for?

I then headed to the Astrology section where I immersed myself in the amazing selection and bought a couple of text books. I also bought a crossword book for my parents, as they love to do crosswords together. After *Powell's*, Robert and I were hungry so we ordered food at *Prasad* and sat out in the Sun. I ordered a Bachelor Bar US$4, a Bunny sly carrot and ginger juice US$5; and the Bhakit raw pasta - zucchini noodles with lemon, basil, cashew alfredo sauce, tomatoes, shredded kale, carrots, broccoli and spinach US$9. Robert ordered an amazing Ganesh Bowl - steamed greens, yellow coconut vegetable curry with cilantro (coriander), sesame seed and lime with quinoa US$9.

After our meal we drove to the *Vendetta* bar where the first part of the *Vida Vegan Con* was taking place: the Meet and Greet. Robert and I met up with various people and made some new friends. I met a lot of people who read my blogs, follow me on *Twitter* and/or are my fans or friends on *FaceBook*, it was really great to put so many faces to names and I'm now even more excited about the conference! We were at the meet and greet for a few hours before we all walked down to the *Curious Comedy Theater* where Marisa's film *Vegucated* was being shown. I had previously seen this in LA at the Animal Rights Conference but was looking forward to seeing it a second time - especially as the theater was sold out! Imber and Mark were there as well, along with various other friends including Jasmin from *Our Hen House*. Robert drove me back to Brittyn's after the documentary finished and I filled her in on the great day Robert and I had together.

Friday 26 August: Hanging out with Alex, Japanese food cart, Vida Vegan Conference & Karaoke

Today I was looking forward to finally meeting Alex Jamieson in person! I had first seen Alex on her then-boyfriend Morgan Spurlock's very popular documentary *Super Size Me*. In the film Morgan mentioned that Alex was a vegan and I could never understand how she would agree to him eating only *McDonald's* food for a month. A few years later Alex released her book *The Great American Detox Diet: Feel Better, Look Better, and Lose Weight by Cleaning Up Your Diet* explaining that she agreed that Morgan could do the film and the diet on the condition that he follow her detox programme afterwards, thus began the writing of her book. Alex's book, along with books *Allergy Cooking with Ease* by Nicolette M Dumke & *Vegan on a Shoestring* by the People's Potato Collective inspired my 2007 *Viva la Vegan!* recipe calendar (now recycled recipe cards) to focus on more alternative foods and grains. My obsession with quinoa began in 2006 when I was researching for my next calendar release.

Alex runs *Delicious Vitality* and we were meant to meet last year when we were both in Portland but it didn't work out. So today Alex picked myself and my luggage up from Brittyn's and we went to the food cart area in Portland to have lunch. We decided on the *Japanese Food Cart* where we bought two tofu dishes US$6 each and shared them. One was the Tofu steak with rice and veg, the other was the Tofu Agadashi with rice and veg. They were both great but we thought brown rice would have been better. After lunch Alex and I found a spot to do our interview.

Alex and I had a great time together, she dropped me off near the *Portland State University Place Hotel* and I walked until I found the exact location - too many one-way streets. This was where the *Vida Vegan Con* was to take place and I was staying with my friend, Anika and her cousin, Arianne. Anika is from Seattle where she runs *Vegan Score* as well as *Lions Share Industries* with her partner, Kirby. I had interviewed both Kirby and Anika last year and had a great time in Seattle last year with them and the rest of the Seattle crew. I did a bit of computer work before Anika arrived, then we hung out for awhile before heading to registration where we got *the best* bag of goodies I've ever seen at *any* event I've been to - and I've been to *a lot!*

That night was the champagne and cupcake reception, where I ate a few cupcakes and drank some non-alcoholic beverages. I also saw Sean who runs the blog *Fat, Gay, Vegan* - another person from Brisbane now living in the UK. I had met Sean and his partner, Josh when Josh had won the *Bake Off* competition for his chocolate chip cookies, at a fundraiser for my first *Green Earth Festival* in 2009. I was looking forward to getting to know Sean better this weekend. I was also looking forward to meeting Stephanie Redcross who runs the vegan marketing website *Vegan Mainstream* and Ryan, who I correspond with regularly, from *T.O.F.U. magazine.*

Even though Anika and I were exhausted after a big day/week, we decided to join the girls at *Suki's bar* along with Arianne for one of my favourite things: karaoke. I was glad we went out as it was a lot of fun. I did a not-so-good rendition of Stevie Nick's *Stand Back* but later on did a great version of Salt-N-Pepa's *Shoop* - it was ever so much fun (Arianne has video footage!) I had always wanted to be Pep when I was at high school and I loved Salt-N-Pepa. It was a late night but well worth it. Jasmin let me down by not coming as she was working on her speech for the next day. We would have been great duetting on *The Trolley Song* by Judy Garland...

Saturday 27 August: My Positive Blogging talk, interview with Jeff, Gala & Mini Mall

In spite of my best intentions to sleep in, I awoke to eat breakfast early. There were pancakes on offer after all. So, I had pancakes and a great chia parfait and some yoghurt. Then we listened to Laura Beck's welcome address as well as the gals from *Vida Vegan Con.* Since I had woken up too early for breakfast, I headed back up to my room to catch up on sleep and then some computer work before lunch. Kathy Peterman took the cutest photo of Jasmin and I with both of our watch rings/ring watches on display. Jasmin and I were separated at birth definitely.

Then I was off to the *Positive Blogging* panel where I was speaking with Christa from *Veggin' Out with Christa*, Gena from *Choosing Raw* & Janessa from *Epicurious Vegan.* I spoke about how I try to keep things positive on my blog, because 1. it's not good ettiquette to speak about others unfavourably especially if you haven't spoken to them first to sort out the situation and 2. some of the places I blog about have no websites of their own and I don't want a negative review of a vegan business to be the first link on an internet search that people see. I also gave some examples of how to speak to restaurants that call themselves vegan but serve honey and about poor customer service. I don't have the comment feature on my blog activated as I don't care what others think of my blog - this statement caused a bit of a ruckus! My blog is just one part of the *Viva la Vegan!* website, not the be all and end all. There were also some great questions from the audience too. See my *YouTube* channel for the video. Kathy Peterman took a great photo of Christa, Gena, Janessa and I after our talk. Gena also blogged about our panel on her *Choosing Raw* website. After our panel I headed to the *Dating & Mating* panel with Anika, it was a bit of fun.

We hung out with Sean who suggested that I get interviewed for the Live video streaming that was happening, and since I'm not one to pass up an opportunity to be on camera, I said "hell, yes!" and Sean took some photos of me in my new dress I bought in Portland with Brittyn. The interview I did live with Jeff is on his *The Cool Vegetarian* website. I had the most people viewing when I was being interviewed live!

After the interview I had a quick chat to Stephanie from *Vegan Mainstream* and then headed upstairs to get ready for the Gala - I was the emcee for the event after all. The gala night was held at the *Ambridge Event Center* so we had to leave the VVC cocoon and venture outside.

There were 350 people at the gala, with food, drinks, a sundae bar and a silent auction with money raised going to *Woodstock Farm Animal Sanctuary* in New York.

There was some great entertainment on the night, including DJ *The Jet Boat Adventurer*; Stephan Nance - who describes himself as *awkwardly charming vegan straight-edge queer alternative piano pop musician* and who reminded me of a young Ben Lee. There was also comedy by Louvella Heartichoke, plus music from Jessica Rose Messern, including her *Vida Vegan* theme song. Robert Cheeke entertained us all on the dance floor with his dancing, and everyone had a great time. I had a few photos taken including one with Ryan & Kira from *T.O.F.U.* magazine, Marisa from *Vegucated*, and with Anika and Arianne.

In one of the corners, there was a photo booth, where you have seven seconds and there are 50+ photos taken of you. It's then put together into a flip book. This was a lot of fun. I was given two books, so I sent one to Peter. You can see my seven seconds of posing, Flip Book-style on my Leigh-Chantelle *YouTube* channel along with my music.

After the gala finished, Anika, Sean, Arianne and I walked to the vegan mini mall as they were all staying open late for us. Chad and crew at *Food Fight Grocery* were very busy, with Nicole and Daniel from *Upton's Naturals* cooking up a feast in the back room. Anika, Sean and Arianne ended up going to drink and socialise with others at *Hungry Tiger Too*. I went to *Scapegoat Tattoo* to get Brian and we lined up for ages to order and wait for our food at *Food Fight*, it was good though. Brian went back to work and I went to *Sweetpea Bakery* to eat my food where Imber and Mark were along with some of their friends. It was *here* that Mark advised me that the Jackalope did in fact not exist, contrary to what Peter had said on our road trip. Hmm, should have trusted my instincts. Mark and Imber walked to *Hungry Tiger Too* with me to see if the girls and Sean were ready to go back to the hotel and since they were not, Mark drove me back. I had planned to go to sleep but ended up uploading my talks to my computer until the girls came back. It was a really fun day and night. I will be tired in the morning.

Sunday 28 August: My Activism panel & Vegan Fashion talks, Goodbyes, Fat Straw & my last night

I shouldn't be up so early, it's ridiculous, but the amazing chia parfait and pancakes are calling me plus my *Activism panel* was starting at 09:40. Mental note: try to get out of any talks in the future that start before 10/11am. It was going to be a long day, as I couldn't have an afternoon nap due to the *Vegan Fashion* panel at 13:45 after lunch. I had also found out this morning from my close school friend, Michelle that one of our mates from school, Andrew had passed away. His funeral would be on Tuesday. I would be back home in Australia the day before so hopefully I will be able to attend.

Jasmin and I headed over to our room for the panel and waited for the others to arrive. I was excited about this panel as I was going to be joined with Jasmin and Ryan. A lot of my activist friends didn't really see the value in a bloggers conference as they thought it was just going to be talking about food and food photography, well it definitely *wasn't*! Jasmin Singer of *Our Hen House* was the moderator and on the panel with me were Ryan Patey of *T.O.F.U. Magazine*, Chelsea Lincoln of *Flavor Vegan*, Sunny Subramanian of *PETA 2 & Vegan Beauty Review* and Isa Chandra Moskowitz of *Post Punk Kitchen*. I was speaking about the various ways I get involved, and encourage others to be involved, in activism with *Viva la Vegan!* and my not-for-profit environmental awareness group, *Green Earth Group* who put on Brisbane's all-vegan festival for the past two years. It was a good panel.

After our panel I caught up on some computer work in the room but didn't have time for a sleep before lunch consisting of a Mexican feast. Next was the *Vegan Fashion* panel with Janessa Philemon-Kerp of *Modified Style & Epicurious Vegan* (our second panel together!) and Anika Ledhe of *Lions Share Industries & Vegan Score*. This was a really great fun and interactive panel and I loved being on a panel with these two ladies. I don't wear or use any non-vegan items whether they are second-hand or not and I would much rather bury the animal who died back into the ground or sell the item online to raise money for an animal charity/sanctuary. I also shop mostly at second-hand and vintage stores and try not to buy items made in countries where sweatshop labour exists or that come from large chain stores. These are just my views. Janessa, Anika and the audience all have different lines that they draw. Kathy Peterman took another cute pic of the panel gals.

Then Anika, Sean and I went to see Jasmin and a few others on the *Opinionated Bloggers* panel before heading to the main room for the closing address by Isa Chandra Moskowitz and Terry Romero. The *VVC* was so organised and well run (how I like things to be) by people who know exactly what they're doing and how to do it. Jess is already talking me into being at the next event in 2013. I'll most likely be there! There are many blogs about the conference, with a *Google Bundle* collection of blogs from the bloggers who attended plus a *Flickr Photo Stream* with many photos, including Gail from *The Hungry Vegan*'s Photo Diary with a cute pic of her and I who I met when I first arrived at the hotel. Thanks to these lovely ladies for putting on such a great event: Jess Scone from *Get Sconed!* & *StumptownVegans.com*, Janessa Philemon-Kerp from *Epicurious Vegan* & *Modified Style* and Michele Truty from *Vegtastic Voyage*.

Most people started leaving, *slowly*, as though they didn't want the weekend to end. I understand completely as this also marks the end of my 2011 US adventures. After 8 weeks here, I'm heading home tomorrow and I really don't want to be. Last year I was ready to leave, this year I'm not at all. Maybe I was looking for a reason to stay this whole time. I have a few. But I also have a lot of work to do from September to December back in Brisbane and interstate so I do actually have to go home now. The first thing I have to do when I get home is attend Andrew's funeral.

I said goodbye to old friends and the great new ones I'd made, had a great chat to Stephanie Redcross from *Vegan Mainstream* and worked out how we can work together in the future. As I was waiting around for Brittyn to pick me up, I had long conversations with Peter and then Holly on the phone. The hotel was getting everything ready for their next event, but it wasn't quiet - there was an accident where someone drove into one of the glass windows!

Brittyn picked me up and we went to get bubble tea at *Fat Straw* before heading back home to her place. We just had some snacks for dinner that night. I filled Brittyn in on the weekend's happenings and gave her some goodies from my goodie bag, it was great to stay with her and hang out with her Mum, Syd, but her cat doesn't seem to think much of me - Corwin still glares at me.

I now have the issue of trying to pack my bag. I have one suitcase, my laptop and a bag with my handbag, video camera, (my tripod *just* broke, today - one less thing to pack!) water bottle etc in it. As I had accumulated a few extra things since getting here 8 weeks ago, it was a bit of a mission to fit everything in plus I didn't really want to have another bag to carry if I didn't have to. Fortunately after taking everything out of my suitcase and rolling all my clothes tightly everything *just fit* into my suitcase. Brittyn didn't think it would work, I didn't really either but I always live in hope. Great! One more sleep. Brittyn and I stayed up talking way too late.

Monday 29 August: PDX, Boise, LAX and the flight home

Syd picked me up and dropped me off at the PDX airport for my flight at 11:45 to Boise where I arrived at 13:45 (1 hour time difference.) I had tacos at a lil' place at the airport for lunch which wasn't that exciting, US$4 ish.

Then I left Boise at 15:20 and arrived at LAX at 16:25. I had a few people I could have organised to hang out with for a few hours before my flight home later that night, but I ended up deciding to stay at the airport. I bought some crisps, pistachios and *Mrs May's* cashews at one of the kiosks to get me through the next few hours. I was aiming on catching up on some work when I was at the airport, but ended up speaking to a lot of my friends, saying goodbye for now and hoping that it wouldn't be long until I saw them again. When I was having a conference call with Nik and Ramy I heard someone say "LC" and I look around and it's my friend Dave from Brisbane (!) who was in LA with other *Supreme Master* initiates for an event a few days ago. I ended up saying goodbye to the guys on the phone and hanging out with

Dave and the others for about half an hour before our flight boarded at 23:55. As always, I had an amazing time on my latest US adventures, and I will miss my friends excessively, but (as they say on reality TV show, *Big Brother*) *it's time to go, Leigh-Chantelle.*

I never really talk to people much on flights, as this is the one time I can sleep really well. I normally sit in the chair, get comfortable and go to sleep for the duration of the flight, only getting up to eat, stretch my legs and go to the bathroom. This time there was a guy on the flight home with me who I ended up chatting with quite a bit, when I was awake. Sean Druitt is a Producer from *Halfbrick Studios* a game development company based in Brisbane who designed the game *Fruit Ninja* that is quite a popular game. Sean was in Seattle at a gaming conference and now heading home to his family. He showed me how to play games on his *iPhone* and I got to play *Fruit Ninja* - I told him this was very vegan-friendly - and *Monster Dash*, something different and fun! On *YouTube* there's this cute video of a cat playing *Fruit Ninja*!

Wednesday 31 August: Home safely in Brisbane, Atomica & Mortality

I arrived safely home at 06:45 Brisbane time. Mum picked me up from the airport and we went to *Atomica* in West End for a vegan tofu scramble.

Tomorrow will be Andrew Porter's funeral at the Gold Coast. We went to school together, had a lot of fun together and he dated a few of my friends. He was 33, a year older than me, and died way too early from cancer when all he wanted to do was fly planes, surf and hang out with his wife and his mates. These sorts of things remind me of why I can't stand pharmaceutical companies, mainstream media, religions and the cancer business. But it also reminds me that people take what they need to get by, like I always say: *whatever gets you through*. Friends, experiences and just life can get us all through just when we need it.

I know so many people on this wonderful world, many of whom I am lucky to call friends, and a select few that are life-long friends. I know who they are and I hope they also know who they are and what they mean to me. Until next time, remember to *love* xx

Links

Leigh-Chantelle:
leigh-chantelle.com
facebook.com/leighchantellefanpage
twitter.com/leighchantelle
gplus.to/leighchantelle
pinterest.com/leighchantelle
myspace.com/leighchantelle
youtube.com/leighchantelle
Music on iTunes: http://itunes.apple.com/us/artist/leigh-chantelle/id340695831

Viva la Vegan!:
vivalavegan.net
facebook.com/vivalavegandotnet
twitter.com/VivaLVegan
gplus.to/VivalaVegan
pinterest.com/vivalavegan
youtube.com/vivalavegandotnet
myspace.com/vivalavegan
Podcasts: http://itunes.apple.com/podcast/viva-la-vegan-s-podcast/id376923451

Green Earth Group:
greenearthgroup.org
greenearthday.net
facebook.com/greenearthgroup
facebook.com/groups/GEGletterwriting
gplus.to/GreenEarthGroup
twitter.com/GreenEarthGrp

All Interviews, Talks & Panels can be found on my *YouTube* channel: youtube.com/
vivalavegandotnet or on the Audio & Visual section of *Viva la Vegan!*: vivalavegan.net/
community/audio-video.html

Restaurants & Food:

Angelica Kitchen - angelicakitchen.com
Araya's Place - arayasplace.com
Atlas Café - atlascafenyc.com/home.html
Babycakes - babycakesnyc.com
Bamboo Garden - bamboogarden.net
Blossom - blossomnyc.com/site/
Blossoming Lotus - blpdx.com
Boca - bocaburger.com
Café Gratitude - cafegratitude.com
Candle 79 - candle79.com
Candle Café - candlecafe.com
Caravan of Dreams - caravanofdreams.net
Chaco Canyon Cafe - chacocanyoncafe.com
Clif Bar - clifbar.com
Community Food Co-Op - bozo.coop
Daiya Foods - daiyafoods.com
Dave's Killer Bread - daveskillerbread.com
Earth Balance - earthbalancenatural.com
Euphoria loves Rawvolution - euphorialovesrawvolution.com
Fat Straw - fatstrawpdx.com
Follow Your Heart - followyourheart.com/market-cafe
Gardein - gardein.com
Georgetown Liquor Company - georgetownliquorcompany.com
Good Food Store - goodfoodstore.com
Healeo - healeo.com
Hemp I Scream - hempiscream.webstarts.com
Home Grown Smoker - homegrownsmoker.wordpress.com
Honest Weight Food Co-Op - hwfc.com
Hungry Tiger Too - hungrytigertoo.com
Jodee's Desserts - jodeesdesserts.com
Kind Kreme - kindkreme.com
LaraBar - larabar.com
Lifethyme Natural Market - lifethymemarket.com
Lula's Sweet Apothecary - lulassweetapothecary.com
M Café de Chaya – mcafedechaya.com
Mighty-O Donuts - mightyo.com
Mrs. May's Naturals - mrsmays.com
Native Foods Café - nativefoods.com
North Coast Co-Op - northcoastco-op.com
Oceana Natural Foods Co-Op - oceanafoods.org
Papa G's - papagees.com
People's Food Co-Op - peoples.coop
Plum Bistro - plumbistro.com
Portobello - portobellopdx.com
Prasad - prasadcuisine.squarespace.com
Real Food Daily - realfood.com
Red & Black Café - redandblackcafe.com
Sacred Chow - sacredchow.com
Sage Organic Vegan Bistro - sageveganbistro.com
Shojin - theshojin.com
Sip Juice Cart - sipjuicecart.com
So Delicious - turtlemountain.com
Soy & Sake - soyandsake.com
St Dames - stdames.com

Sticky Fingers Bakery - stickyfingersbakery.com
Stogo - stogonyc.com
Sunflower Vegetarian Restaurant - crystalsunflower.com
Sun Power Natural Café - suncafe.com
Sweet Lemon Vegan Bistro - sweetlemonveggiebistro.com
Sweet Pea Bakery - sweetpeabaking.com
Taco del Mar - tacodelmar.com
Taco del Sol - tacodelsolhelena.com
Terri - terrinyc.com
Thrive - generationthrive.com
Tofurky - tofurky.com
Tofutti - tofutti.com
Upton's Naturals - uptonsnaturals.com
Vegan Cakes by Jenny Mac - vegancakesbyjennymac.com
Vegan Shortcake - veganshortcake.com
Vegetarian House - vegetarianhouse.com
Vege Thai - vegethai.com
The Veggie Grill - veggiegrill.com
Verite Catering - veritecatering.com
The V-Spot - spreadvegan.com
WaterCourse Foods - watercoursefoods.com
Wayward Vegan Café - waywardvegancafe.com
Wild Wood - wildwoodfoods.com
X's to O's Bakery - xoxoveganbakery.com
Z Pizza - zpizza.com

Friends:
Animal Liberation Frontline (previously Voice of the Voiceless) - animalliberationfrontline.com
Animal Rescue Corps - animalrescuecorps.org
Animal Rescue Media Education (ARME) - arme.tv
ARZone - arzone.ning.com
A Virtually Mindful Assistant - avirtuallymindfulassistant.com
The Beagle Freedom Project - beaglefreedomproject.org
Bold Native - boldnative.com
Brian T Wilson - btwilsontattoos.com
Button Makers - buttonmakers.net
Chic Vegan - chicvegan.com
Clara's Cakes - claracakes.com
Delicious Vitality - deliciousvitality.com
The Discerning Brute - thediscerningbrute.com
Evolotus PR - evolotuspr.com
The Faded - thefaded.com
Fat, Gay, Vegan - fatgayvegan.com
Food Fight Grocery - foodfightgrocery.com
Food Not Bombs - foodnotbombs.net
Galapagos Preservation Society - gpsociety.org
Gather Films (previously Open Road Films) - gatherfilms.net
Green is the New Red - greenisthenewred.com
Happy Cow - happycow.net
Joaquin Pastor on IMDB - imdb.com/name/nm2789447
Lion's Share Industries - lionsshareindustries.com
Live Natural Live Well - livenaturallivewell.com
Masxs - masxsonbothsides.com
Motive Company - motivecompany.com
Nik Tyler on IMDB - imdb.com/name/nm2273331

Obsessive Compulsive Cosmetics - occmakeup.com
Oh Tragic Vinyl Night - ohtragicvinylnight.com
On A Dollar A Day - dollaradaybook.com
The Only Sparkle - theonlysparkle.com
Open Road Films - gatherfilms.net
Our Hen House - ourhenhouse.org
Paunchiest - paunchiest.com
Pixie Portraits - pixieportraits.net
Rebecca Bolte Photography - rebeccabolte.com
Scapegoat Tattoo - scapegoattattoo.com
Skin Trade - skintradethemovie.com
The Sparrow Project - sparrowmedia.net
Spork Online - sporkonline.com
Stop Animal Exploitation Now (SAEN) - all-creatures.org/saen/index.html
The Thinking Vegan - thethinkingvegan.com
T.O.F.U. Magazine - tofu.limitedpressing.com & ilovetofu.ca
Uncaged Films - uncagedfilms.com
Vaute Couture - vautecouture.com
Vegan Body Building & Fitness - veganbodybuilding.com
Vegan Mainstream - veganmainstream.com
Vegan Score - veganscore.com
Vegina - vegina.net
Vegucated - getvegucated.com
Voice of the Voiceless - animalliberationfrontline.com
Warcry Communications - warcrycommunications.com
Win Animal Rights (WAR) - facebook.com/WinAnimalRights
Yogatography - yogatography.tumblr.com

Others:

Amtrak - amtrak.com
Animal Acres - animalacres.org
Animal Rights Conference - arconference.org
Band of Mercy - bandofmercy.org
Beacon's Closet - beaconscloset.com
Bluestockings - bluestockings.com
Brooklyn Superhero Supply Company - superherosupplies.com
The Chocolate Shoebox - thechocolateshoebox.com
Devil's Tower - devilstowerkoa.com
Earthlings - earthlings.com
Experimental Media & Performing Arts Center (EMPAC) - empac.rpi.edu
Farm Animal Rights Movement (FARM) - farmusa.org
Fliptography - fliptography.net
Food Allergy - food-allergy.org
Fred Meyer - fredmeyer.com
Georgetown Records - georgetownrecords.net
Half Brick - halfbrick.com
Humane Party - humaneparty.net
Humboldt Redwoods State Park - humboldtredwoods.org
Institute for Humane Education - humaneeducation.org
International Vegetarian Union - ivu.org
Lewis & Clark - law.lclark.edu
Megabus - us.megabus.com
Moo Shoes - mooshoes.com
People's Potato Collective - peoplespotato.weebly.com
Pigs Peace Sanctuary - pigspeace.org
PSI of Oregon - psioforegon.com
Powell's Books - powells.com
Sidecar for Pigs Peace - sidecarforpigspeace.com
Spook Cave - spookcave.com
Super Shuttle - supershuttle.com
Supreme Master Ching Hai Association - godsdirectcontact.org
Trader Joe's - traderjoes.com
Unity - unitythemovie.com
Vegan Wares - veganwares.com.au
Veg News - vegnews.com
Vida Vegan Con - vidavegancon.com
 (All the bloggers from Vida Vegan Con: vidavegancon.com/2011-vvc/speakers)
 (Live Stream videos see: livestream.com/vidaveganconlive)
Whole Foods Market - wholefoodsmarket.com
Woodstock Farm Animal Sanctuary - woodstocksanctuary.org
911 Truth - 911truth.org

Please note: all of these links were working as of February 2012,
please do an internet search if any of them are broken.

About the Author

Leigh-Chantelle lives mostly in sunny Brisbane, Australia where she runs the online vegan community vivalavegan.net, the not-for-profit environmental awareness *Green Earth Group*, as well as coordinates Online Etiquette Education and Social Media Marketing with *Epicentre Equilibrium*. Leigh-Chantelle believes in the rights of all beings, networking, surrounding herself with people on the same life path as her and she is a bit obsessed with quinoa.

Leigh-Chantelle is an accredited Naturopath, Nutritionist and Western Herbalist who combines her passion for vegan health along with her natural therapies and healing skills. Leigh-Chantelle has released three *Viva la Vegan!* recipe calendars, a plant-based Detox Diet e-book as well as re-released her recipe calendars as recycled recipe cards. Over the past 15 years since Leigh-Chantelle has been a vegan she has been involved as a sponsor, performer, speaker, emcee and stallholder for various animal rights, vegan, vegetarian, environmental and cruelty-free fundraisers, forums, conferences, festivals and events throughout Australia and internationally.

Leigh-Chantelle is available for select speaking engagements, seminars, panel discussions and readings on the following:

- Veganism, Animal Rights and Activism
- Staging Effective Events, Engaging Volunteers and Team Work
- Online Etiquette, Social Media Marketing and Online Skills

To enquire about a possible appearance, please contact email@vivalavegan.net

You can find Leigh-Chantelle, Viva la Vegan!, Green Earth Group and Epicentre Equilibrium on

facebook. **twitter** You**Tube** **8+** **iTunes**

Viva la Vegan! started to promote Leigh-Chantelle's Recipe Calendars in 2005 and has since grown to be an interactive community for vegans focusing on positive education, information and vegan outreach. Through the vivalavegan.net website, Leigh-Chantelle's focus is on educating people to alternative lifestyle choices, proving that via compassion we can heal ourselves and each other. Vivalavegan.net focuses on easy to prepare recipes; blogs, articles and podcasts; interactive forum, informative and how-to videos, interviews with inspiring vegans, vegan mentoring and much more.

vivalavegan.net

Other Books by Leigh-Chantelle:

What Do Vegans Eat?

ISBN 978-0-9808484-0-3
Digtial ISBN 978-0-9808484-1-0

2012

www.ingramcontent.com/pod-product-compliance
Lightning Source LLC
Chambersburg PA
CBHW072047040426
42447CB00012BB/3054